WALKING
IN THE LIGHT

WALKING
IN THE LIGHT

R. PEARSALL SMITH
and
HANNAH WHITALL SMITH

FRANCIS ASBURY PRESS
of Zondervan Publishing House

Grand Rapids. Michigan

WALKING IN THE LIGHT

Copyright © 1986 by the Zondervan Corporation
Grand Rapids, Michigan

FRANCIS ASBURY PRESS is an imprint of
Zondervan Publishing House
1415 Lake Drive, S.E.
Grand Rapids, Michigan 49506

Library of Congress Cataloging in Publication Data
Smith, Robert Pearsall, 1827–1898.
    Walking in the light.

      1. Christian life. I. Smith, Hannah Whitall, 1832–1911.
II. Title.
BV4501.S687 1986   248.4   86–22456
ISBN 0-310-20921-8

Designed by Louise Bauer
Edited by Joseph D. Allison

Printed in the United States of America

86 87 88 89 90 91 / 9 8 7 6 5 4 3 2 1

CONTENTS

FOREWORD

THE TRIUMPH AND TRAGEDY
OF ROBERT PEARSALL SMITH

The republication of R. Pearsall Smith's little volume, *Walking in the Light*, more than one hundred years after its original printing is an event of no little consequence and one that calls for some explanation. This book normally should have been reprinted at regular intervals over the years, along with much of the other standard literature of the holiness revival of the last century. R. Pearsall Smith was certainly one of the most significant evangelists of the renewal movement that swept America, England, and the European continent in the 1870s and 1880s. During his active ministry, he strongly influenced many who were rising to leadership in Evangelicalism. But his impact was more like that of a blazing meteor than of a steady light. As a formative influence in the revival, he was there powerfully for seven years; and then suddenly—he was gone!

The unusual nature and limited duration of his ministry has relegated the few publications that he authored to years of neglect. Furthermore, he was noted more for the power of his presence as a platform speaker or small-group participant than as a writer; the writings of his talented wife, Hannah Whitall Smith, overshadowed his own.

But he remains a person of unusual significance for the history of revivalism, because the abiding results of his brief ministry are dramatic. God used his staccato-like burst of spiritual life to move thousands of Christians out of their old lives of continuing spiritual defeat into new lives of victory over sin and power for more effective witness.

Smith's message—the message of *Walking in the Light*—was the proclamation of "holiness now by faith." It set the late-nineteenth-century Evangelicals of England and the European continent (largely Calvinist in theology) on fire with new expectations about the nature of the normal Christian life. The brief story that follows will provide some insight into his rise, his fall, and why (in spite of that unusual sequence of events) we can still profit from reading Smith's message, which proved to be so life-changing for those who have felt his influence. We may understand more clearly why he was able to guide thousands of pilgrims on the quest to know God's perfect will, although his ministry ended in great disappointment to his friends and great personal tragedy for his family.

A mood of frustration and pessimism pervaded the churches of Europe by the last quarter of the nineteenth century. The causes of this spiritual malaise were many and complex. The French were depressed by their losses to Prussia in the war that ended in 1870. In Germany, the victors also experienced frustration, while the much-heralded national revival of religion that was anticipated in the wake of the victory failed to develop. In England, the Evangelical cause was waning; its leaders had lost much of the zeal that had marked the great social reforms of earlier coalitions which the movement had forged. The Anglo-Catholic/Broad Church/Evangelical struggles had sapped the energies of the established Church of England. Large Free Church pulpits such as Charles Spurgeon's Tabernacle continued to draw impressive crowds; but the political and cultural influence of English Evangelicals—even of the giants such as Spurgeon—did not really affect the centers of power that were shaping the future of the nation.

Perhaps most important of all, new secular theologies and theories of social change were confronting the traditional understandings of the evangelical faith. The challenge was especially threatening to those in Victorian Evangelicalism who tended to separate faith from everyday life, who pictured the Christian life under the "poor worm" paradigm, and who promoted a severe separation of the church from the world.

It was almost by accident that R. Pearsall Smith found his way to England in 1873 and became caught up in a budding revival movement which promised to invade all sectors of the Evangelical community there. The renowned American evangelist Dwight L. Moody had set the tone for the revival, calling sinners to "come home" to a loving Father. For their part, Smith and his colleagues William Boardman and Asa Mahan brought a message of renewal for professing Christians, as they challenged them to experience a fresh baptism of the Holy Spirit that would result in a more consistent Christian witness to an increasingly agnostic world. Moody himself sensed the critical importance of Smith's contribution to the revival. He telegraphed personal words of greeting to Smith's 1875 Meeting for the Promotion of Scriptural Holiness at Brighton, England. Moody told Smith and the church leaders gathered with him that he considered their meeting to be one of the most significant in the history of the church since the time of the apostles.

Who was this lay evangelist, praised so freely, who was so strategic to God's work in his time and yet so vaguely remembered in the history of Christian renewal? That question opens up one of the lesser known chapters of the history of evangelical Christianity. As we have already hinted, it is a remarkable story of how God can use a flawed instrument to carry out His own purposes in the church.

The author of *Walking in the Light* was born a birthright Philadelphia Quaker in 1827. His family's American ancestry came down from James Logan, personal secretary to the founder of Pennsylvania, William Penn. Because of Logan's generosity, the family had birthright to the titular headship of the Philadelphia public library corporation. This provided the family with a certain established social status in the city, as they preserved that renowned collection which had been built around the original grant of books by their family's progenitor.

In 1851 Pearsall married one of the most eligible young Quaker women in Philadelphia, Hannah Tatum Whitall. She was also a birthright Quaker, a member of Philadelphia's Arch Street Friends Yearly Meeting. Her father owned one of the premier manufacturing businesses of the day, the Whitall-Tatum glass plant of Millville, New Jersey. The staid religious customs of the Friends did not satisfy the spiritual aspirations of the young couple. A deep restlessness for a more intimate personal relationship with God marked both of their lives. These longings were satisfied during two great surges of spiritual renewal which bracketed the American Civil War. The first was the Fulton Street (N.Y.C.) Revival, or Layman's Revival, of 1857–58. In that "Year of Miracle," as it has come to be known in American religious history, both Pearsall and Hannah experienced new birth in Christ as the renewal moved through the religious communities of Philadelphia. Subsequently, their association with the Quakers began to cool. Robert turned toward Presbyterianism and Hannah associated herself with the Plymouth Brethren who had helped her into the kingdom of God.

But it was during the second surge of renewal and among the Methodists that the Smiths found the deeper relationship with God which they had been seeking. In July of 1867 a group of Methodist Episcopal ministers who were increasingly troubled by the declining spirituality of their denomination called all persons who were interested in a deeper Christian commitment to gather in the city park at Vineland, New Jersey, for a ten-day camp meeting. This meeting would be specifically dedicated to teaching about the experience of Christian perfection (or "entire sanctification," as American Methodists commonly referred to it). The Smiths had already become aware of the experience through their contacts with Methodist employees at the family's glass factory in Millville, where Robert served as manager. And the camp meeting site was familiar territory to them: Friends lived in Vineland and the Smiths' Philadelphia home was within convenient range, either by carriage or by the new rail line that passed through Millville from Philadelphia on its way to the ocean resorts.

So the Smiths were among almost twenty thousand people who crowded the temporary religious community set up in the heart of Vineland that summer. In the course of the meetings, Pearsall responded to the call to entire sanctification. With many others who have entered into this total consecration to the disposition to God's will, he was emotionally moved. Hannah, always more intellectually oriented than he, struggled with her doubts until the third National Association camp meeting held in the summer of 1869 at Round Lake, New York. Then she too testified to the experience of sanctification, although she sensed none of the emotional release which had accompanied Pearsall's crisis of faith. For years thereafter, she yearned for the strongly affective internal witness that her husband had felt; but her longings were never fulfilled. Firmly convinced of the faithfulness of God and the reliability of His Word, she maintained a wholehearted commitment to God from that moment until her death in 1911. But only toward the end of her life, far removed from camp meetings and her intimate involvement in holiness evangelism, could Hannah acknowledge that her experiences of God in those early meetings had marked the most moving spiritual encounters of her life.

The message of *Walking in the Light* was born out of these early experiences of the Smiths and their contacts with Methodist revivalists such as John Inskip and Alfred Cookman. The Methodist "second blessing" teaching—that a crisis of faith subsequent to justification and the new birth will cleanse the heart from the old "bent to sinning" and set it free to love God completely—was the motivating idea of this revival. The evangelists offered their hearers the possibility of a life of daily victory if they would receive the fullness of the Holy Spirit and continue in a moment-by-moment trust in Christ. Pearsall Smith cast this simple truth in non-theological language, then preached it with compelling urgency to the most learned theologians and the most poorly informed laypersons; to members of state churches and free churches. His message was the same for all: that anyone could put into daily practice the fundamental truth of the gospel—that "Jesus saves me *now*."

Robert Pearsall Smith sought to preach that truth in terms familiar to non-Wesleyan ears in order to assure a wider hearing for his message. By design, he and his companions sought to separate the teaching from any hint of perfectionism. To the Calvinists who constituted the larger part of their English and European audiences, the word *perfection* inevitably conveyed only one meaning—"sinless perfection" or "absolute perfection." To such individuals, the very idea of Christian perfection faintly veiled a set of goals that were unattainable for any Christian this side of glory.

This difficulty still clouds the dialogue over sanctification between Calvinists and Wesleyans. The unique pattern of Reformed theology seems to make it very difficult for those who understand the Scriptures within a Calvinistic framework to conceive of the possibility of Christian perfection, such as lies at the heart of the Wesleyan understanding of God's election and grace.

A recognition of this tension between two fundamentally different interpretations of biblical truth is essential to our account; for the perfectionism that Smith and Boardman tried so assiduously to remove from the teaching they had received from their Methodist brothers and sisters was still present in their Higher Life message. Like a spectre, it caused many who read or heard their teaching to hesitate in joining their "second blessing" crusade. Eventually, when Smith's own failures became known, it was far easier for many of his English and European sponsors to rationalize the precipitous manner in which they forsook him. They believed any teaching of perfectionism would carry its adherents along the path to antinomianism; and, regrettably, Pearsall Smith's personal difficulties appeared to confirm both their fears and their logic.

Wealthy, winsome, vigorous, vocal, and unable to say no to the many requests for evangelistic engagements that followed his sanctification experience in 1867, Pearsall Smith's physical and psychological reserves had been rapidly depleted. The measure of those resources had always been scant; a blow to his head while horseback riding had left permanent damage to his nervous system. Furthermore, the manic-depressive nature that had plagued his family became more and more evident as the pressures of his overburdened evangelistic schedule multiplied. The sudden death of his son with typhoid fever in 1872 aggravated his already tenuous situation.

With the help of his physician, Hannah got him to agree to break his demanding schedule and take a recreational trip to Egypt. On his way there, Smith stopped in England in 1873 for a brief series of social visits which were recommended to him by mutual friends. The testimony of his sanctification experience was always on his lips. As a result, it was not long before a series of meetings were set up by his new English contacts. These meetings plunged him into the revival milieu that was already developing among British Evangelicals of every theological stripe.

His ability to interpret his essentially Wesleyan message to such a varied audience proved to be unusually effective. Eventually, he persuaded Hannah to join him in England with their children; as co-evangelists, the Smiths drew larger and larger crowds while the scope of their influence among church leaders in Europe broadened. In the spring of 1875, Pearsall Smith took the churches of Germany, France, and Holland by storm. He gained a hearing for his Higher Life message even among the established Reformed and Lutheran churches in Germany. The emperor's own church in Berlin was made available for his meetings when the smaller pietist meeting halls would not accommodate the crowds. The Reformed movement of France became deeply involved in his ministry as the Monod family gave him their support. In his mostly negative commentary on Smith's ministry,[1] the Princeton scholar and committed Calvinist B. B. Warfield called this brief surge of European evangelism one of the most dynamic since Pentecost.

After his swing through the European continent, Smith came back to Brighton, England, for the meeting of May 1875 that we mentioned previously. There about ten thousand British, Dutch, French, Swiss, and German pastors listened to the holiness teaching of the Smiths, Boardman, Mahan, and other American evangelists. The common testimony of those who attended was that it had caused a turnabout in their understanding of the life of Christian holiness. A note of faith and expectation had replaced the pessimism and defeat that had characterized many of their lives.

---

[1] B. B. Warfield, *Perfectionism*, vol. 2 (New York: Oxford University, 1932), chap. 4.

The momentum of spiritual renewal that began in Pearsall Smith's meetings still exerts a positive influence on Christian spirituality and the evangelical mission of the church. The centers of German Lutheran and Reformed pietism were reinvigorated by his ministry. The German Inner-City Mission Movement found renewed vigor for its social and evangelistic ministries. The Keswick Movement of England became the most direct heir of Smith's basic teachings. A surge of new interest in overseas missionary work resulted from Keswick and related movements, which have provided thousands of mission recruits and tapped new resources for their support. Keswick became a center for the renewal of the evangelical wing of the Church of England. Dwight L. Moody and R. L. Torrey embraced Keswick's Higher Life vision and brought its message back to many of the evangelical Calvinistic churches in America which had hesitated to accept the doctrine as they perceived it in its original Methodist context. Evangelical Calvinist schools such as Moody, Dallas, Columbia, and Biola still are marked by the truth, as are the Pentecostal denominations such as the Assemblies of God.

The message of the Higher Life Movement endured, but its messenger faltered and ultimately failed. Brighton, the triumph of Smith's message, was also Brighton, the tragedy of the messenger. In little more than a month after the close of that meeting, the Smith family was on its way back to America, broken and bewildered. Rumors of Pearsall Smith's doctrinal and moral irregularities had brought about his sudden dismissal by his English sponsors. The facts as we have them today, after more than one hundred years of inquiry, support their cause for concern; but from our present vantage point, we may question whether the Brighton committee had to deal with Smith in such a precipitous manner. In view of Smith's own claim to innocence and the steady, lifelong affirmation of his integrity by Hannah (who never brooked duplicity), it seems that a more redemptive stance could have been taken.

It appears that Pearsall Smith's teachings of a "bridal mysticism" that centered around the relationship between Christ as Husband and Bridegroom to the Christian—particularly Christian women—were taking on sensual overtones. As Smith responded to the demands for spiritual direction that constantly flooded his day, he often referred to this conjugal symbolism.[2] When called to account, Smith recognized his errors and sought the forgiveness and counsel of his sponsors. But their additional concerns for his Arminian-oriented teachings made them feel that a more radical solution was best for their cause and the cause of the revival. So this incident brought about his abrupt dismissal from the European evangelistic circuit.

Smith's American friends and supporters disagreed with the judgment of the English leaders; they sought to save him and his ministry for the Higher Life Movement. But Smith's meager physical and emotional reserves had been totally depleted by three years of unremitting evangelistic work. From the Brighton incident until his death in 1899, his spiritual decline was steady. He never again testified to spiritual peace and died a pathetic, defeated man.

Hannah, on the other hand, quickly recovered her

---

[2] Editor's Note: This led to charges of moral indiscretion in Smith's private counseling of a young lady. See Marie Henry, *The Private Life of Hannah Whitall Smith* (Grand Rapids: Chosen, 1984), chap. 8.

spiritual equilibrium. In spite of this personal tragedy, she continued to influence the churches and the world through her widely-read books and her avid leadership in the causes of temperance reform and women's suffrage.

So what are we to say, left as we are with this perplexing puzzle of the life and ministry of the author? Final knowledge of his personal culpability and how readily he may have responded to God's efforts to restore him is beyond our understanding or our responsibility. God only knows whether the accusations were true. In spite of our dilemma at that point, however, we are left with one very clear theological statement: *The ministry of God's Word is ultimately in God's own hand, and we often are puzzled by how He brings His will to pass.* In this instance, as in so many less spectacular instances in Christian history, His truth comes through in spite of personal weakness in His human instrument.

God used R. Pearsall Smith, always vulnerable and finally faulted, to bring enduring spiritual renewal to significant elements of the church. The message of this book has more than proven its worth in the renewal it has generated in the church, from the time Smith preached it and wrote it until the present day. May this little volume encourage thousands more to make the total personal surrender to Christ which it teaches. Every Christian who comes to experience the truth that "Jesus saves me *now*," and who continues to trust in Christ only, may realize the life of assurance and love, victory and power, that God clearly promises us by His indwelling Spirit.

MELVIN E. DIETER
ASBURY THEOLOGICAL SEMINARY

PREFACE

In a former work, *Holiness through Faith*, I sought to show from the Scriptures, illustrated by the experiences of Christians, that the promises of God warrant our claiming an inwrought practical holiness through Christ, as well as an imputed completeness in Him; that these promises of grace are ever larger than His commands to be holy; that notwithstanding all the imperfections and infirmities of our condition, we may through the "obedience of faith" gain Enoch's testimony that we "please God"; and that the power of this victory is faith, and faith only.

These pages, however, are especially addressed to those who have already realized this overcoming faith, and this conscious soul union with the Lord, the experience sometimes described by the term "the higher Christian life." Such people practically understand the limitations of my meaning, when I speak of "abiding in Christ," "deliverance from sin," "the rest of faith," "full salvation," "Christ formed within," or "walking in the Spirit." However, lest I be misunderstood by anyone, I would here ask that the terms used in this book be interpreted by a brief statement of what we mean when we speak of "walking in the light," and of the consequent "cleansing from all sin."

He walks in the light of God who without evasion brings every action, emotion, and thought into the all-searching light of the presence of God. What the light reveals as evil, the soul rejects, and so "our fellowship is with the Father, and with His Son Jesus Christ," (1 John 1:3), a fellowship in light. A walk in the light always leads to the blood of Christ, and all that the light shows of evil in our nature becomes effectually cleansed by the blood.

"If we say that we have fellowship with him, and walk in darkness, we lie, and do not the truth: but if we walk in the light, as he is in the light, we have fellowship one with another, and the blood of Jesus Christ his Son cleanseth us from all sin" (1 John 1:6–7).

It is clear that these words were not addressed to an unconverted sinner; such a one is never told to walk in the light and have fellowship with God before his sins can be pardoned. Neither is it intended for a backslider, for the epistle is written "that your joy may be full" and "that ye sin not" (1 John 1:4; 2:1). The passage surely teaches that we are not only to be justified from our *sins*, but also to be inwardly cleansed "from all *sin*" (v. 7, italics added), that deep evil of our nature that is antecedent to sins or sinning. Absolute discernment of what evil is cannot be imparted to us in our present dim twilight of knowledge. The angels in the perfection of their faculties or Adam in his innocence might perceive the true moral character of their every emotion and action, but we cannot. God does not require of our faculties, so sadly darkened by the Fall, a perfect knowledge; but He does both ask and impart to faith a perfect love, the full devotion of our hearts, such as they are in all their imperfection and weakness. That shortcoming which is not contrary to knowledge or love* is not imputed to us and is fully met by the atoning blood of Jesus.

It is evident that there are many things not according to the perfect holiness of God in the life of the sanctified believer, things that in the early dawn have not yet been discovered to it. As the light increases, more and more is exposed of the remaining evil, and the soul continues to be practically cleansed by the blood. In what sense this unseen, unknown evil is or is not *sin*, I leave as a theological question, and use the term in its generally understood meaning—"that which brings a sense of condemnation or impurity." Practically, I find myself with "a conscience [or knowledge] void of offense" (Acts 24:16); and "if our heart condemn us not, then have we confidence toward God" (I John 3:21). Though we have not an absolute, unconditional sinlessness, it is an incalculable blessing and strength to every believer to have a happy heart, free from all known sin, a heart now able to accept the consciousness that Christ does indeed cleanse from all sin and dwell in the purified temple of our being. To this, faith brought us. In this, faith keeps us. A lapse of faith would restore our old condition of conscious inward evil and outward trespass.

At this point of highest privilege is also the pinnacle of greatest danger. If we say that we have an inherent holiness, or "if we say that we have no sin," otherwise than as the blood of Christ momentarily

---

*"Love is the fulfilling of the law." Study carefully Matthew 22:37; Mark 12:30–33; Luke 10:27; John 13:34; 15:12; Romans 5:5; 13:9–10; Galatians 5:6, 18; Ephesians 1:4; 1 John 2:23; 3; 4:7, 12, 16.

cleanses us, "we deceive ourselves, and the truth is not in us" (I John 1:8). Such a delusion is a denial of our need for Christ, the assertion of a self-wrought holiness, and a clothing of ourselves in the filthy rags of our own righteousness, which are ruinous to our souls and loathsome to God.

Even angels found sin and ruin when they ceased to depend on God's sustaining power. My condition is far below that of angels. I am under the shadow of sin through Adam, and of its development into sins by my own wickedness. There is a poison of sin in my human condition, which the cleansing blood of Christ can neutralize moment by moment. I have an inherent proclivity to corruption, which the blood can overcome by the energy of His life and health. I am without knowledge in myself, and so it is the work of the guiding Spirit to make me wise. Thus, in the blood of Christ I find cleansing and life, and in His Spirit I find direction through every moment in which my faith takes Christ for wisdom. Each day reveals more and more of the wonders of grace that are in Christ Jesus, and in Him alone.

It is no small pleasure to embody in this book two chapters written by my wife. Converted to God the same day as I, she has, by her daily counsels and communion, opened the pathway of faith and holiness to my steps.

R. Pearsall Smith

WALKING
IN THE LIGHT

WALKING
IN THE LIGHT

HERE does the Scripture indicate that definite experience known as "the Sabbath of the soul," or "the abiding inward rest," in the enjoyment of which continuous victory over the world is possible? I cannot deny (it would not be candid to do so) the reality of such a life in Christ, which I have witnessed or known in others; nor would I deny that it corresponds with the Scripture standards of Christian privilege. If testimony proves anything, it proves a range and elevation of Christian experience. . .such as I have not obtained. And yet I do not see it defined as a *distinct* experience in the Scriptures."

Such was the candid question put to me a few days ago by a most earnest and intelligent Christian, a minister presiding over an important school for Christian workers, honestly desiring to know the truth of God and to live it.

The reply was at once suggested, "The proof is everywhere! Definite and uniform victory over evil is taught everywhere in Scripture where Christian experience is dealt with. It permeates the whole doctrine of Scripture. It is the only normal life recognized by the Bible, and anything short of it is the exception. It is easier to define the character of a voyage to one who is making it, than to one who is only desiring to do so or has scarcely decided to venture for the first time upon the water. The experience of trusting the ocean; the wonderful deliverances when the ship, like a mere shell, lies in the great surging deep; and the secured results of the voyage can be definite only to him who has ventured his life upon the sea. So it is that only those who have fully cast themselves upon the promises of God can realize how complete and definite is their preservation from evil."

A CLEAN HEART CREATED

In its simplest form, we find evidence of this definite experience in the words that follow the royal backslider's cry for pardon: "Have mercy upon me, O God" (Ps. 51:1) and "Blot out my transgressions" (Ps. 51:10) are followed by the prayer, "Create in me a clean heart, O God; and renew a right spirit within me." Surely, any of us will know definitely when a pure, holy, and clean heart is created within us. Most Christians say that it is not in them. But a few who have long said this now testify that they have received in answer to the prayer of faith a heart *fully* cleansed by the blood of Jesus from the consciousness of inward defilement and passion. This destiny is definitely stated by Scripture: "If we walk in the light, as he is in the light, we have fellowship one with another, and the blood of Jesus Christ his Son cleanseth us from all sin"

(I John 1:7). It is definitely realized in the experience of a Christian who has begun to walk in the wonderful light and fellowship of God and the inward cleansing of Christ's blood. A heart that can *without effort* meet sarcasm and reproach with a divinely given love and gentleness; a heart that does not answer to the calls of passion and finds, both in the agitating emergencies of life and in the hourly minor trials of domestic intercourse, an undisturbed inward calm has reached a definite experience of the cleansing of His blood.

ABIDING IN CHRIST

Most people who profess to be Christians, while conscious of loving the Lord Jesus and desiring to obey Him, are also painfully aware that they do not abide in Him in the same manner in which a branch abides in the vine. They know that they have not proved that word, "If a man love me, he will keep my words: and my Father will love him, and we will come unto him, and make our abode with him" (John 14:23). They have known at seasons the presence of the Father and the Son, but they have not yet realized the permanence of God's *abode* within them. Now this is a definite promise of Scripture, no less definite in its realization by the child of God than when he claims any other promise in entire consecration and trust. To him the promises affixed to "abiding in Christ" are now definitely realized—the sinning no more, the much fruit, and the answered prayers (1 John 3:6; John 15:5, 7).

WALKING IN THE SPIRIT

Walking in the Spirit, with its pledged results of not fulfilling the lusts of the flesh, is a definite condition of the soul. The withering of the works of the flesh and the bearing of the fruit of the Spirit form a definite experience beyond any mistake of the consciousness. "Love, joy, peace, long-suffering, gentleness, goodness, faith, meekness, temperance" (Gal. 5:22) are not characteristic of an indefinite dreamy condition of the soul, but the outflow of a cleansed heart, consciously and definitely received by the believer through faith.

REST

To use another term, it is definite "rest" to the soul when, having put away many weights, it has at length laid aside the very last one and has risen to God in perfect freedom. The soul can now run with patience the race set before it, because it is freed from burdens and looks *only* to Jesus who, having been the divine Author of its faith, is also the Finisher of it. The heart to which Jesus has given rest from the guilt of sin can now, in its entire abandonment to Him, assume the yoke of obedience without reserve or qualification and find that, unresisted, it no longer galls. The soul has definitely come to Christ. It has with equal definiteness bowed beneath His yoke in meekness and lowliness of heart, finding the second rest that He promised in a deep inward Sabbath-keeping of the soul. The first rest Jesus *gives* to the weary burden-bearer, while the second is *found* by the meek and lowly yoke-bearer.

If we examine the history of the children of Israel, we find that the wilderness gave them no true rest. It witnessed a continual succession of backslidings in the very presence of the tabernacle, with all of its provisions for pardon and cleansing. The wilderness was not the fulfillment of God's promise to Abraham, but the consequence of limiting the Holy One of Israel at Kadesh-barnea in His power to give victory over God's enemies. However, it was a definite experience of rest when the Israelites left behind them the wilderness, trusted Jehovah in the person of Joshua (the forerunner of Jesus), and crossed the Jordan in triumph. It is no less a definite experience of rest when the Christian, who has long wandered in the wilderness of sinning and repenting, at length abandons the reproach of Egyptian worldliness and enters into the rest prepared for the people of God, the soul's inward Sabbath, in unlimited consecration and trust.

DEATH AND RESURRECTION

In no part of Scripture is this Christian experience stated more clearly than in the sixth chapter of Romans. It describes, not the deliverance of the Red Sea over again, but the life across the Jordan. It meets the all-important question of whether the redeemed shall continue to sin, and shows that our only refuge from the horrid workings of inward corruption is to be found in our *realized* crucifixion with Christ, "that the body of sin might be destroyed, that henceforth we should not serve sin" (v. 6).

"Christ crucified for us" has been preached with a blessed and almost unparalleled distinctness in recent years. But now the mission of the church is to preach with no less emphasis and distinctness the Christian's crucifixion with Christ and his deadness to sin, with the consequent life of righteousness.

DELIVERANCE

In Romans 7 we read of the experience of a Christian who turned back to walk for a time in the wilderness of spiritual failure. It is the experience of a true Christian, though not a true Christian experience. It is only necessary to observe how exactly it reflects the common condition of too many of the redeemed (vv. 10–24) in order to decide to whom it applies. He whom it represents is indeed a "wretched man," so long as he finds himself in captivity to the law of sin—continually grieving Him whom his soul loves. But how definitely does the way of deliverance open to his gaze in reply to his exclamation of need: "O wretched man that I am! who shall deliver me?" Christ, once clasped in the soul's extremity of need for pardon, is now again embraced in its agony of desire for deliverance from inward corruption.

The eighth chapter of Romans describes as definite an experience of victory as the seventh chapter was definite in failure. No transition in all of Scripture, save conversion, is so clearly marked as this soul crisis at the vision of Christ as the Deliverer from sinning.

As the experience of condemnation described in Romans 3 culminated in the charge, "For all have sinned, and come short of the glory of God" (v. 23), followed in the same sentence by the declaration of our release through Christ Jesus, so the description of indwelling sin in Romans 7 culminates in the exclamation of bondage and agony, "O wretched man that I am! who shall deliver me from the body of this death?" And it is followed in the same breath by the joyful cry, "I thank God through Jesus Christ our Lord" (v. 25). He is at once, and by the same way of faith, our

Deliverer from the condemnation and bondage of sin. Romans 8 describes as definite a triumph over sinfulness as Romans 4–5 describe triumph over condemnation for sinning.

CHRIST FORMED WITHIN

It was no indefinite, general thought of progress that filled the soul of Paul when he groaned that Christ might be formed in the hearts of the Galatian converts. And when he told them that he did not himself frustrate, by any self-imposed barriers, the grace of God, he gave them the key to experiencing the life of Christ within themselves: "I am crucified with Christ: nevertheless I live; yet not I, but Christ liveth in me: and the life which I now live in the flesh I live by the faith of the Son of God, who loved me, and gave himself for me"(Gal. 2:20).

A YOUNG CONVERT'S QUESTION

As he sat in a railway car, an intelligent young man who had just begun to read the Scriptures daily, but to whom they were as yet an enigma, was led to see that salvation is through faith only and in Christ alone. He trusted Christ for pardon and realized that in believing he became the possessor of eternal life. After a few minutes' solemn pause, he asked, "But will this trust in Christ keep me from sinning?"

The answer was, "Definite faith in Christ for pardon frees your soul from the load of guilt and condemnation that has weighed upon you, and it has a *tendency* to make sin hateful to you. But to correct the bias of your nature toward sin, your faith must receive

Christ definitely in another of His relations to your soul. You must come to Him in full consecration to receive effectual inward cleansing by His blood. You have just learned to trust Jesus to blot out your iniquities, and He has done it. Now, with this lesson fresh before you, come to Him for a clean heart within and a full victory without. Can you doubt that, having saved your soul from death, He is ready to keep your feet from falling? 'As ye have therefore received Christ Jesus the Lord, so walk ye in him' (Col. 2:6)."

It would seem as definite an experience to trust Christ for holiness of heart as for pardon. George Müller could definitely trust the living God to supply nearly two thousand souls under his care with their temporal needs day by day. Cannot a child of God trust Christ as definitely to supply one poor, weak, but confiding heart with all it needs of holiness from moment to moment? The evil Herodias claimed the king's promise, and he dared not refuse to give her even half his kingdom (Matt. 14:1–11). Is God less to be trusted? Are His promises of cleansing and preservation from evil to His saints who will trust them less secure than those of pardon to the sinner who will trust them? Is not the power of God pledged to the keeping of God's family as fully as to the forgiveness of the repentant wanderer? All the attributes of God are involved in the smallest of His pledges to the least of His trusting children. Happiest is he who most perfectly honors God by committing himself to the inviolable "I will" of a covenant-keeping God.

WAVERING FAITH

WAVERING FAITH

By Hannah Whitall Smith

OD'S unalterable plan in all of His dealings with the souls of men and women is, "According to your faith be it unto you" (Matt. 9:29). The awakened sinner, seeking the forgiveness of sins, may wrestle, agonize, and plead with all the fervor and earnestness of which he is capable; but until he believes in the forgiveness of God, he cannot find peace. God does not deal with the sinner according to the fervor of his wrestlings or pleadings, but according to his faith. The moment he has faith to be saved, he is saved, and not until then. This is because God's salvation is not a purchase to be made, nor wages to be earned, nor a summit to be climbed, nor a height to be attained, but simply a *gift* to be received. And nothing but faith can receive a gift from God.

But if this is God's rule with regard to the poor awakened sinner, how much more must it be the rule regarding His own family, who have been born of the Spirit and upon whom He has bestowed all the riches that are in Christ. To them most assuredly His word is, "What things soever ye desire, when ye pray, believe that ye receive them, and ye shall have them" (Mark 11:24).

When therefore the child of God begins to be dissatisfied with the failing, halting experience that is the too general condition of the church and begins to hunger and thirst after that higher life of victory, that abiding rest that he sees some other Christians enjoying and that he realizes his privilege also, what is the necessary condition to his entering into that blessed experience? The first condition of course is consecration, because none but the fully consecrated can fully believe. In order for the Lord Jesus to heal us of our sins, we must be willing to be healed; we must give ourselves up to His healing power. But I presuppose all of this and address only the souls that are conscious of being fully given up to the Lord, as far as they have light to see. And surely to such the rule applies with even greater power than to the unconverted (if that could be) that according to their faith it shall be unto them.

But this principle is not always clearly recognized, and the result is that many longing souls are delayed for months, even years, from entering the land of rest whose borders they have long before reached.

Satan understands this matter perfectly. He knows what God's plan is, and therefore his principal attacks are directed against our *faith*, and he knows how to come in such garb as completely to deceive the unsuspecting soul. First, he occupies the soul with itself, with its own goodness or badness, with its feelings, its fervor, or its coldness; thus, he effectually hinders it from looking at Jesus and seeing in Him a Savior who is able to save to the very uttermost. Second, when the believer has been brought out of this snare and enabled for a blessed moment to take a definite step of faith and to cast himself wholly upon the Lord Jesus, believing that He does receive him and does indeed save him from the power of sin as well as from the guilt of his sins, Satan endeavors to make this faith a wavering, intermittent faith, and thus effectually hinders the believer's onward progress or increasing light. It is of this point especially that I desire to write just now, because I am sure that much of the unsatisfactory experience of those who have really entered the higher Christian life arises from this cause.

I address myself therefore to the dissatisfied rather than to the seekers. You have sought and found this rest in Christ at one time and for a while you rejoiced in it greatly. But a cloud seems to have come over your experience, and you cannot discover what has brought it. Your spiritual sky is not clear. Your communion with God is interrupted. Your victories are intermittent. Yet you are not conscious of having taken back any part of your consecration to Him, nor of indulging anything contrary to His will.

If this is not the case, and you feel some want of conformity to the will of God, then of course I am not addressing you; for you there is one step absolutely necessary before you can take any other. You must get on believing ground again, the ground of entire consecration to God. But you know this, and I need not elaborate.

I am addressing those who desire above everything else to be altogether the Lord's, but who seem to find a veil that hides the fullness of Christ from their gaze, and thus are hungry and thirsty in the very presence of God's perfect supply. To such I can only say, "According to your faith be it unto you."

Your difficulties arise from the wavering character of your faith. You do not hold the beginning of your confidence steadfast to the end. You have not believed steadfastly that which you believed at first. The definite trust in the Lord Jesus, which you exercised then and which brought you such wonderful victory and rest, has become indefinite and uncertain. Satan has been turning your attention to yourself. He says to you, "Look at your heart and at your life. See how cold you are, how indifferent, how far from being what you ought to be. How can you for a moment dare to believe that Jesus saves *you*, and makes you holy?" You have listened to him and, turning your eyes off Jesus, have begun to doubt. Your very doubts have produced the results you dreaded. Jesus cannot fully save a doubting soul. Remember this. And the moment you find yourself beginning to doubt, stop short and think of what will be the inevitable consequences.

If you doubt Him, your consecration is fruitless, your efforts are unavailing, your pleadings are unanswered. God has said that unless we ask in faith, nothing doubting, we need not think to receive anything from Him. Doubt is fatal. And yet, so completely has Satan blinded your eyes on this point that you look upon doubt as an almost necessary condition of your nature. How often we have heard children of God say, "I am such a doubter," as though this peculiar weakness excused them for all of their other shortcomings. We never hear a Christian say, "I am such a liar," and make that excuse for his failures. And yet, in the sight of God, to doubt is as displeasing as to lie; sometimes I think it must be more so, because it is so dishonoring to His faithfulness. No form of wickedness ever hindered the Lord Jesus from doing His mighty works except the wickedness of unbelief. And you, dear Christian, are as completely hindering His mighty work in your soul by your unbelief as the Samaritans hindered Him by theirs. I am sure that if you realized this, you would not dare to doubt. Do you think that God has made a mistake, and that the Christian who doubts *can* receive something from the Lord? Have you not invariably found that doubting brings you into darkness and unrest, and finally into sin?

But you ask, "How then can I get rid of this doubting?" I will tell you. Consecrate your power of believing to the Lord Jesus, just as you have consecrated all of your other powers, and trust Him to keep you trusting. You have so absolutely yielded yourself up to the Lord that you would not dare to disobey Him. Yield yourself to believe His Word regarding faith in the same absolute and irrevocable way, and you will feel that neither do you dare to doubt. Make your believing as inevitable and necessary as your obedience is. You would obey God, I believe, even though you should die in the act. Believe Him also, even though the effort to believe should cost you your life. The conflict may be very severe; it may seem at times unendurable. But let your unchanging declaration be, "I will not suffer myself to doubt. I choose to believe."

When Satan comes with his suggestions of doubt, meet him with more positive assertions of your faith. I say, "when Satan comes," because all doubts are from him, and all discouragements. The Holy Spirit never suggests doubt or discouragement to any soul. Never!

Settle this matter in your mind, and you will find the way to victory is wonderfully cleared. Your doubts are all from Satan, and you know he has been a liar from the beginning. Do not give heed to them therefore, even for a moment. Turn from them with horror, as you would from blasphemy. You cannot help their being suggested to you, as you cannot help hearing the swearing of boys along the street; but you can stop listening to the boys, and you can equally well stop listening to these suggestions of doubt. A very practical way to baffle Satan in this matter is to go at once and confess to someone your faith that Jesus does save you now fully and that His blood cleanses you from all unrighteousness. If this is not possible, write your declaration of faith in a letter, or confess it aloud to yourself and to God. Satan always flees when the precious blood of Christ is trusted and confessed. But however you do it, make sure that you will never doubt again. According to your faith it shall be unto you; and while you are trusting Jesus to save you from sinning and to make you pure in heart, He is absolutely pledged to do it. He cannot fail. "What things soever ye desire, when ye pray, believe that ye receive them, and ye shall have them" (Mark 11:24).

I want to be very practical in explaining this, because I am sure many hearts are bowed down in secret from this fatal habit of doubting. I am convinced that many of my readers could testify to the truth of this. They know that their wavering faith is the cause of their wavering experience. One day they believed that Jesus did indeed save them from sin and from sinning, and it has been so in their experience. But the next day they looked at themselves and began to doubt, so their experience has corresponded to their doubts. If this is your problem, let all doubting be past. Start out on a path of unwavering, steady faith. Believe steadfastly, through everything, no matter what comes, just as you believed upon your entering into this blessed "higher life," and never doubt it again. If the step of faith you took then was to reckon yourself dead to sin, continue thus to reckon without wavering. If it was to believe that the blessed blood of Jesus cleansed you from all unrighteousness, go on believing this, steadily and without compromise. Or if your step of faith was simply to accept that Jesus saved you fully, exercise that same faith now and keep exercising it continually, without intermission. Whatever your first step of faith may have been, continue in it steadfast, for "we are made partakers of Christ, if we hold the beginning of our confidence steadfast unto the end" (Heb. 3:14). There is no other way. Let nothing shake your faith. Should even sin overtake you, you must not doubt. On the discovery of it, take 1 John 1:9 and act on it: "If we confess our sins, he is faithful and just to forgive us our sins, and to cleanse us from all unrighteousness." Confess your sin immediately upon the discovery of it; believe at once that God does forgive it and does cleanse you again from all unrighteousness, and go on believing it. Believe it more firmly than ever. Believe it because He says it, not because you feel it or see it. Believe it whether you feel it or not. Believe it even when you seem to be believing something that is absolutely untrue. Believe it actively and persistently, and according to your faith it shall be unto you.

Oh, that my words could save any doubting soul from its sad and weary experiences! My heart yearns over such people with a tender sympathy. I know how sincere you are, and how hard you struggle to reach the experience of abiding in Christ, which your conscience tells you is the only state that is truly satisfying for the Christian. I know also how the fatal habit of doubting effectually holds you back. In order to have abiding rest, you must have abiding faith. An intermittent faith always brings intermittent rest. Will you learn this lesson?

Would that I could write in letters of light before your eyes God's unalterable rule: *According to your faith it shall be unto you*!

PROGRESS

PROGRESS

HE expectation of some people concerning the walk of the redeemed, who through faith have begun their journey on the "highway of holiness" (Isa. 35:8, para.), is that it is not a *way* but a *place* without further progress in the divine life. They suppose it is a place secured from the assaults of temptation, where there is little need to take heed lest they fall and where there is a uniform flow of intense feelings of joy. Truly, we have found the hindrances removed from an endless progression in the divine life; but we have found that Satan uses his most potent resources against those who are within the citadel, to draw them out if possible. We walk by faith only, and if our faith fails, we stumble. Though, on the one hand, we rejoice in the Savior's presence and His smile of favor, we at the same time suffer in filling up "that which is behind of the afflictions of Christ" (Col. 1:24), especially His sorrow in beholding the perishing multitudes around us and the faithlessness of the professing church. We are anxious—soberly, sincerely, and without exaggeration—to set before the believer who has commenced a life of full union with Christ the progress, dangers, and trials of the resurrection life.

So much has been written about how one enters the highway of holiness that I fear this highway may seem like a succession of beginnings. There is a continual advance and many distinct stages of progress in this walk of faith; nevertheless, the entrance is best likened to the Israelites' crossing the Jordan out of Egypt. Alas, so many have seen the grapes of Eshcol (Num. 13:23–24; 32:9; Deut. 1:24)—they have heard the united testimonies of those who have spied out the land and have been urged to enter the Promised Land immediately—but they have shrunk back and failed to obtain the rest that remains for the people of God! The rest remains indeed, they argue, for those who are specially gifted to receive it, "but not for me." They forget that all distinctions between people have been obliterated in God's sight, first by their common ruin and then by the common grace opened to all by the cross of Christ. Such people would be the first to answer a similar argument in regard to the forgiveness of sins; but they strangely cling to their unbelief and the alleged impossibility of their ever entering into rest. Once more entreating them to allow no apology for their condition, we would speak a little to those who, having believed, "do enter into rest"(Heb. 4:3).

Although we look forward to the time when the church, the bride of Christ, shall find rest in her Lord's bosom—when Israel shall rest in the land under the rule of Messiah and all of creation shall rest from its groaning—yet there is a present rest of the soul (Heb. 4:9) into which many believers have entered by faith.

Self has ceased to be the center of its own little world, and One worthy of being worshiped has become the absorbing object of the believer's affections, existence, and hopes. As the poet expressed of an earthly affection:

> *Love took up the harp of life*
> *And smote on all the chords with might;*
> *Smote the chord of Self that, trembling,*
> *Passed in music out of sight.*

The soul of such a person is learning the lesson of forgetting self and all that is left behind. The vision of Jesus has put away the believer's sins, and his own human righteousness vanishes before it. The light of day not only dispels the darkness but hides the stars that shone in the darkness. Not only are past sins forgotten but every ground of self-confidence and the soul's past progress, for it is reaching ever forward toward the prize of the high calling of God in Christ Jesus.

As the Christian advances on this highway of holiness, occupied with thoughts of Jesus rather than with temptation or sin, he assumes the simplicity of a child who does not analyze his emotions but with naturalness gives play to them. Gone are the *effort* to love and the self-reproach of the heart for its wandering affections, for the soul has learned to dwell in love and thus to dwell in God (1 John 4:16). This rest may not fully come at once, when the soul first finds victory over the world; it results from walking in the Spirit and it grows imperceptibly as a holy habit in the Christian, who becomes conscious of it by its results rather than by any effort toward its attainment. If effort there be, it is the effort to cease from one's own works, that one may enter into rest.

Thus, the Christian becomes as a little child trained in the kingdom of heaven, which consists of righteousness, peace, and joy in the Holy Spirit. He knows his deliverance from the power of darkness and his translation into the kingdom of God's dear Son as present, inward, realized facts. He finds the accomplishment of that promise, "He that hath my commandments, and keepeth them, he it is that loveth me: and he that loveth me shall be loved of my Father, and I will love him, and will manifest myself to him" (John 14:21). A holy *intimacy* with Jesus is formed, leading to a constant intercourse with Him as real as that with the dearest of earthly friends and intimately more satisfying. With a heart purified by faith, the Christian now "pure in heart" finds his vision no longer occupied with the world, self, and sin. He sees God and is occupied with Christ. Beyond even this manifestation of God, the soul knows the Father and the Son in the sober certainty of a consciousness that becomes the reality of the promise, "My Father will love him, and we will come unto him, and make our abode with him" (John 14:23). An *abode* is a permanent dwelling place. "I bear within me the divine verity of the triune God," an eminent Christian once said; and nothing short of this fulfills the Word of God and the eternal purposes of our redemption.

Christian progress is not necessarily a constant succession of stumblings and risings, an endless soiling and recleansing of the garments. He who said, "Thy sins are forgiven thee," can as easily say also, "Rise up and walk." He who washed us whiter than snow is able to preserve us from defiling the garments that He has bestowed upon us. As we experience more and more that Jesus is able to keep those who are committed to

Him, our spirit of fear is replaced by the spirit "of power, and of love, and of a sound mind" (2 Tim. 1:7). Putting on the new man, "which after God is created in righteousness and true holiness," (Eph. 4:24), our hearts are open to receive the assurances of the love of Jesus with the same freedom and simplicity with which we received the assurance of His pardon. While our heart was conscious of any separation from God, it was slow to apprehend any expression of affection and tender sympathy from Christ. As one writer has described it:

> If these affections be not understood as passing between Christ and the saint, if we do not without reserve allow this satisfaction with each other, our souls will not enter into much of that communion which the Scripture provides for. We should allow and entertain the thought of Christ's delight in the saints with *the same certainty* that we allow the thought of His having purchased and sanctified them by His blood. But this communion must spring from intelligence of the soul, or it will be mere natural fervor. . . .
>
> The love of kindred warrants the deepest intimacies. There is ease in coming in and going out [with our relatives]. Expressions of joy are not deemed intrusive, nay, are sanctioned as due and comely. The heart knows its right to indulge itself over its object, and that without check or shame. This is the glory of this affection, the richest feast of the heart. It is the *persons*, not their qualities, that form the ground of our love for our kindred. It is *himself* that the heart embraces, not His sorrows, favors, or excellencies.
>
> Do we believe this? Does it make us happy? We are naturally suspicious of any efforts to make us happy in God, because our moral sense, our natural conscience, tells us of having lost all right to even His ordinary

blessings. The mere moral sense will therefore be quick to stand to [i.e., resist] it, and question all overtures of peace from heaven, and be ready to challenge their reality. *Faith* gainsays these conclusions of nature. It refuses at times to think according to the moral sense of nature. . . .In the revelation of God, faith reads our abundant title to be near Him, and be happy with Him, though natural conscience and our sense of the fitness of things would have it otherwise. Faith feeds where the natural sensibilities of the natural mind would count it presumption to tread.

Do we ponder without suspicion or reserve the thoughts of such love toward us in the heart of Jesus? Does it make us happy? How are we to meet this way of Jesus' heart to us?

But now, in the consciousness of the cleansing of His blood, we launch out on the boundless ocean of the love of God. We come to "know the love of Christ," while we are yet conscious that it "passeth knowledge" (Eph. 3:19). Hungering and thirsting for righteousness, we have come to Jesus and been filled; and yet never did we know such "quenchless yearnings for a holier life." We are "perfect," yet not already perfected; "satisfied," yet hungering and thirsting; "at rest," and yet earnestly contending; "knowing" the love of Christ, yet panting to comprehend what is its breadth and length, depth and height; "always rejoicing," yet sorrowful. Our inward knowledge of God involves all these paradoxes of His Word. God multiplies His blessings where there is faith to receive them, so that yesterday's privileges seem but as the twilight before the dawn, verifying the word that "the path of the just is as the shining light, that shineth more and more unto the perfect day" (Prov. 4:18).

Service for Jesus has now become not only a happy freedom, but a sacred joy; it is done for Him whose eye alone the heart now cares for. Our rejoicing over the found sheep is sanctified by the higher and more sacred privilege of sharing the joy of the Shepherd. Our intercessory prayer becomes the *attitude* rather than the effort of the soul; in self-forgetfulness the heart prays "without ceasing" and draws down the blessings of God upon all around it. Of self-sacrifice or self-effort our soul almost loses consciousness, for the affections that cling to what should be sacrificed are withered and replaced by a soul-absorbing union with Jesus. The judgment of those around us loses both its restraining and its stimulating effect as our heart realizes that it has "none to please but Jesus."

His approval satisfies all the desires of our heart. What a wonderful calmness this gives in the simplest conversation or the public meeting, under circumstances of overwhelming responsibility before the largest audiences! All sense of loneliness is gone, be the surroundings a desert or a crowd, since Jesus is present in the soul; and the heart finds in His constant company not satiety but increasing joy. These heavenly privileges are multiplied through the faith that no longer expects a break in the current of its holy intimacy with Jesus, but an increase from day to day and year to year. We turn a deaf ear to those who limit "the Holy One of Israel" (Ps. 78:41) in His grace and gifts. We expect—and confidently anticipate—His continually increasing blessings. We listen to the voice that Israel would not heed: "I am the LORD thy God, which brought thee out of the land of Egypt: *open thy mouth wide, and I will fill it*" (Ps. 81:10, italics added). Our soul has brought all its tithes into God's storehouse and now finds the windows of heaven opened so that the poor vessel sometimes feels that it has not enough room to contain all the blessings now poured out. It no longer speaks of its own desires as separate from the will of God, but finds an inward conformity to Him who works in the soul *to will* as well as to do of His good pleasure. The sounds of the world grow fainter and more distant as the melody of heaven occupies our heart more exclusively. Even the active callings of life cannot destroy this divine fellowship, for faith is above all circumstances. His love cannot be quenched by many waters, neither can floods drown it.

Our painfully insufficient words cannot convey what the realization of this union with Jesus is to the soul. I have been blessed by having the ties of human affection toward those nearest me in life sealed by our fellowship in Jesus; but no union of purpose, no unrestraint of soul, no abandonment of heart in the intercourse of human affection could equal the sacred intimacy that I find in my Lord and Savior. Nor is the deep sense of this reality exceeded in any outward intercourse with those nearest and dearest in life. Sooner would I doubt the evidences of my senses than the Spirit's witnessing directly with my spirit that I belong to Christ.

In redeeming us out of the world by His own blood, Christ ordained that there should be nothing short of full union of heart with Him for those "elect according to the foreknowledge of God the Father, through sanctification of the Spirit, *unto obedience* and sprinkling of the blood of Jesus," (1 Peter 1:2, italics added), and "who *are* kept by the power of God through faith" (1 Peter 1:5, italics added). How much of privilege, joy, and reward will be missed by those who turn away from the fullness of this union with Jesus because they think this is impossible for them!

When the Christian has thus become buried by baptism into death to the world and self, and has found himself risen with Christ, he is able to walk in that newness of life in which old things are passed away and all things have become new. He is no longer occupied with the contemplation of sin and is not expecting to trespass. Yet even the victory over sin and self is but the negative part of sanctification. The positive work is found in the affections of the soul which, having the hindrances of a habit of sinning removed, can be filled by the Spirit and thus fitted for a work beyond all of its natural capacities. Kept by grace through faith in the risen Savior, we can set no limit on what God may accomplish in a believer who loses his own life for Jesus' sake and finds the life of Christ filling his soul.

The song of holy triumph is a "song of degrees," so in setting forth these privileges we would have no one be discouraged, because these privileges herald only the dawning of the day of full deliverance. We must await the time when the Sun of Righteousness will arise with effectual healing in His wings. Thus, what Augustine says of love may be applied to this walk of full trust in Jesus:

> Is love made perfect the moment it is born? So far from it, it is born in order that it may be brought to perfection. When it has been born, it is nourished; when it has been nourished, it is strengthened; when it has been strengthened, it is made perfect.

Let us set our standard of Christian privilege as high as God has set it in His Word. Let us cry, "Lord, increase our faith!" And let us be *willing to have it increased according to God's measure.*

DANGERS

DANGERS

T MAY seem strange to speak of dangers in the walk with Christ, for it is essentially a walk of safety; indeed, it is the *only* place of true safety. Christ is our fortress. In Him we are beyond the range of the Enemy's arrows. The danger, however, is not in our position "in Christ," but in our liability to be drawn out of Him by sudden temptation or by lying disguises—by Satan's transformation into an angel of light, or by the various forms of the "sleight of men, and cunning craftiness, whereby they lie in wait to deceive" (Eph. 4:14). The Devil, with his thousands of years' experience in deceiving mankind, is a formidable adversary. The world presents to us not only gross temptation but many fair shows of religiosity that would deceive. And the flesh or "body of sin," though dead as we live in Christ, may revive its activity by our want of continued refuge in the resurrection life.

And should we leave our strong Tower, none would be more liable to outward trespass than we, who have abandoned even the failing reeds of self-effort. The world, the flesh, and the Devil are all against us. In a world where nearly everyone distrusts God, people who are utterly self-helpless yet triumphant through God are a spectacle for the heavenly hosts—and a special mark for the darts of Satan.

Even in the vigorous youth of the early church, founded under the guidance of the apostles themselves, the leaven of corruption began to work. The Roman Christians had to be cautioned not to judge their brethren unfairly. The Corinthians failed to purge moral sin from their midst. The Galatians, having begun in the life of the Spirit, tried to be made perfect by the laws of the flesh. The apostle Paul warned the Philippians not to become enemies of the Cross, minding earthly things. And the Colossians seem to have considered a return to the rudiments of the world.

However, a special admonition was given to the Ephesian church, which appears to have been living in resurrection power more than any other church: "Put on the whole armor of God," urged the apostle, "that ye may be able to stand against the wiles of the Devil. For we wrestle not against flesh and blood, but against. . .spiritual wickedness in high places" (Eph. 6:11–12). The contest was not so much with the appetites, as in the wilderness on the other side of Jordan before God's people entered their Promised Land. Indeed, now the whole armor of God was needed—the omission of a single piece was dangerous—because the contest had moved to higher ground, where the Christians needed all the equipment that God had given them for victory. Yet they were not so safe when they met their Amalekite enemies in the wilderness as now, when they had the whole armor of God available to meet the Philistine in his more appalling manifestations.

Conscious that God's truth, revealed through the Word, is girded about our loins; that not only an imputed but an imparted righteousness gives us the "answer of a good conscience" (1 Peter 3:21); that we have our feet shod with the preparation of the gospel that brings God's peace to our souls; that the shield of faith not only should but *actually does* turn the fiery darts of the Wicked One; that realized, present salvation is our helmet of protection; and that we wield the sword of victorious power, which we have proven by experience—we now find ourselves praying always in the Spirit and watching with all perseverance. Here is danger indeed; but here is victory too.

I have experienced conflict with Satan for ten days at a time, so actual as to remind me of Luther's vivid description of his contest in the castle. It was not a conflict of temptation through the senses, but a conflict for retaining possession of my resurrection life and victory. No one who has been through such conflicts will speak lightly of them, nor of the danger of resting in the memory of the victory, instead of in Christ alone. Continual practice with the weak human heart since the days of Adam has taught Satan the temptation suited to each soul. The danger is real, though the situation may be far removed from the old scenes of the believer's wilderness defeats. No less real is the victory of faith.

Our duty of confessing Christ in all the things that He bestows upon us is essentially connected with retaining His blessings, including the knowledge that we are forgiven of our sins and the assurance that we are inwardly cleansed of sin, which is a vital part of salvation. The special blessing of God rests upon our confession; yet, like other blessings that lie near concealed dangers, the confession of what Christ is to us (1 Cor. 1:30) may be turned by Satan into a profession of what we are *in ourselves*. In a moment, the righteousness of the saint may be turned to filthy rags, even to pollution itself.

How instantly a believer is turned to darkness and doubt if he entertains the Devil's suggestion that the forgiveness of his sins is partly of good works and the remainder of faith. This is true even if, like Simon Zelotes, he makes the most abject confession of his unworthiness along with his claim of merit for his self-inflicted penance. "Salvation is of the Lord," wholly and exclusively of the Lord; nor will He in any point share its glory with any human being. As His enemies hated Christ, though no cause for their hatred could be found in the Blessed One, so God saved us without any cause or merit being found in ourselves. When there was nothing in our character or behavior that God could approve, He loved us freely and created in us that which was of His own holiness—and which alone He could love. So those who are most confident of the remission of their sins are most emphatic in testifying that it is purely due to the grace of God. The danger lies in being tempted to assume that self played a part in the work of redemption.

We find a wonderful parallel in the work of inward cleansing which ought always to follow the forgiveness of sins. The instant that we detect the faintest thought of self-merit lodging in our souls, we should heed the warning of Malachi 2:

> If ye will not hear, and if ye will not lay it to heart, to give glory unto my name, saith the LORD of hosts, I will even send a curse upon you, and *I will curse your blessings:* yea, I have cursed them already, because ye do not lay it to heart (v. 2, italics added).

Such awful words of warning these are! May we take them to heart while we yet "believe unto righteousness"—imparted as well as imputed righteousness—and confess unto a full salvation, exclaiming, "Come and hear, all ye that fear God, and I will declare what he hath done for my soul" (Ps. 66:16). Thus, as in the forgiveness of sins, we shall glory in the Lord alone and be led like Paul to say, "I have therefore whereof I may glory through Jesus Christ" (Rom. 15:17).

After long acquaintance with many Christians who attribute to Christ the glory for setting up His kingdom in their hearts, I believe none are so truly humble and distrustful of themselves or work so unfeignedly to give God all the glory for His work. None are so free from legalism, even in cases where their precise statements of doctrine differ from their free language of prayer or praise to God. As they acknowledge their confidence in Christ for the forgiveness of their sins (which once seemed to them a statement of self-exaltation), just so they have found true humility in confessing what God has done for their souls in sanctification.

A fatal danger of this highway is that, having found the practical righteousness which comes by faith and having realized how much it is to be preferred to our former experience as Christians, our confidence may be shifted unconsciously from a dependence on Christ to a confidence in our own attainment. Even though it was first received as a free gift, this condition may at length seem an achievement of our own. With such a change of understanding, we lose touch with the root of our experience; and though the branch may appear unchanged for a time, it must eventually be cut off if not restored. Christ must be our soul's perpetual center. If He is not the center, self will take His place, and each of His precious gifts will be turned into a curse. We are called to glory, not by self-glorying, but by glorifying God in our bodies and our spirits, which are God's.

To the question, "Which is the most dangerous doctrine?" a saint replied, "God's truth held carnally and to exalt self." No fall can be so tragic as that from the height of full communion with God to the depth of this sin, robbing Christ of His glory in our lives. The believer enlightened by the Spirit and accustomed to discerning between good and evil will, at the first moment he is conscious of this temptation, fly to Jesus and cry, "Deliver [me] from the snare of the fowler" (Ps. 91:2)! Such a person will not pray uncertainly, but in the joyous confidence of victory—a confidence that will be honored by God.

There will be danger everywhere while Satan is yet unchained. And there is danger in being so preoccupied with the superstructure of our relationship with God that we lose sight of the foundation upon which it is laid. We may not deny that the foundation is there, but we may fail to keep the structure planted squarely upon it. The mercy seat of Christ must be kept continually in view. In this regard, many earnest seekers after holiness have failed. In this regard, some of the most excellent people have missed their full privileges. A walk in the light of God does not cleanse us of sin; but it brings us to the blood of Christ, which effectually cleanses us from all sin.

THE SPIRIT'S ROLE

For good reason, the Holy Spirit is placed between "the riches of the glory of his inheritance in the saints" (Eph. 1:18) and being "filled with all the fullness of God" (Eph. 3:19). The second chapter of Ephesians humbles us by recalling our former death in trespasses and sins, when the living Spirit raised us up to "sit together in heavenly places in Christ Jesus" (Eph. 2:6). Also, for good reason, this chapter emphasizes that our salvation is "by grace. . .through faith. . .not of [ourselves]. . .the gift of God. . .not of works" (vv. 8–9). If our lives on earth continued for many ages, we must attribute to the blood of Christ the forgiveness of our past. And we must attribute to His blood our present inward cleansing. Not only is His blood needful to wash away our defilement; it prevents further defilement by sin. A pebble by the roadside is often soiled and the rains wash it clean again; but if it is placed in a sparkling stream, it does not become defiled again. So by faith

> *We every moment have*
> *The merit of His blood.*

We would not be truly consecrated to God's priesthood if the blood was omitted from our consecration. The Old Testament order of priestly consecration was *first* the blood, *then* the oil; so it is still. God's order for His priests is the blood for pardon, the Spirit to enlighten; the blood for cleansing, the Spirit to fill the temple that has been cleansed.

Therefore, we solemnly warn any who believe they are walking the highway of holiness that Satan has the power to transform himself into an angel of light and deceive them into betraying their Lord. The old superstition that Satan flees at the sign of the cross, like many other fictions, has a foundation in truth: When the Christian finds himself continually living in the sight of Calvary, yet risen with Christ in a life of resurrection power, he cannot go astray. The cross separates him from self-righteousness as effectually as from other sins and sinning. All those who err, either in doctrine or in experience, lose sight of Calvary before yielding themselves to the guidance of Satan. But by being constantly mindful of the Atonement, that large class of Christians remains "dead indeed unto sin" and "risen with Christ."

Christ is our Gibraltar. In Him, we are safe; outside Him, we are weaker than other people. No arrows can penetrate our Rock and strong Tower. If we are pierced by them, it is because we no longer abide in Him.

May God be praised that we find in Christ sufficient provision for our safety and victory! Let us be sure that by prayer and faithful living we avail ourselves of His provision, not sometimes, but *always*.

HOLY HABITS
OF SOUL

HOLY HABITS
OF SOUL

HEN God makes His own clear, searching light to shine into the most remote corners of our hearts, revealing the remnants of old evils which, though restrained in expression, still dwell within our souls, He not only cleanses us with the blood of Christ but also begins to form *holy habits* within us.

It is a great grace to be restrained from sin; but it is a greater grace to find accomplished within us the promise, "I will. . .consume thy filthiness out of thee" (Ezek. 22:15). Truly, our God is a consuming fire. He says, "I will turn my hand upon thee, and purely purge away thy dross" (Isa. 1:25). Yet His work within us does not end with this emptying, cleansing process. The cleansed temple of our soul is to become the dwelling of the living God. His presence brings us into harmony with Him, so that He does indeed work in us "both *to will* and to do of his good pleasure" (Phil. 2:13, italics added). He stays the crosscurrents within us and allows the peace of our inward life to flow on "like a river." Yet there remain old habits—operative by the powerful law of accustomed successions of thought— that must be changed. Indeed, the power of habit must be applied to the new life of sanctification now opened before the soul, as powerfully as it once bore upon the life of habitual failure. Let us see in what way this law of our being, which we call *habit*, can become a channel of blessing in our new life.

LIVING OUT OF SIGHT OF SIN

We often find within ourselves the habit of looking at sin and pondering the probability of its return, when we should be concerned with Christ and the things that are true, honest, just, pure, lovely, and of good report. The apostle Paul admonishes us in this regard, "If there be any virtue, and if there be any praise, think on these things" (Phil. 4:8). By so doing, we shall not occupy the soul about things that are untrue, impure, or unlovely.

Let all of us who have "risen with Christ" in an actual newness of life see to it that we habitually *live in the atmosphere of the kingdom*, which is righteousness, peace, and joy in the Holy Spirit. Then, if we are compelled to deal with sin in the world or the church, we shall be able to do it as those to whom "all things. . . are pure" (Rom. 14:20) or undefiling. Reckoning ourselves to be "dead indeed unto sin, but alive unto God" (Rom. 6:11), we must habitually "follow after the things which make for peace, and things wherewith one may edify another" (Rom. 14:19). The mind's occupation with sin is the first step toward committing sin; but our Father in His mercy would have us so entirely delivered from the power of darkness and so consciously translated into the kingdom of His dear Son that the things suitable for the kingdom should *exclusively* occupy our souls. Furthermore, He wills that things belonging to the power of darkness should be put out of our sight, as much as is possible in this scene of conflict.

Well do I remember the joyous rest that spread through my soul when, long after I had learned the importance of living the resurrection life, I began to form the habit of living *out of sight of sin*, wholly occupying my soul with the things of God. Before that time, dwelling in love and dwelling in God, far above the malarious breath of sin, often occupied my thoughts when I began to muse on the possibility of sin. But when I began to cultivate this new habit of living, a veil seemed to be drawn over my past; my life became a succession of "henceforths," as I looked forward without any *expectation* of sinning again. This made me very tender to the leadings of God. I cannot say that there has been no trespass since. But I have never lived so near to Christ, with so little in my heart condemning me. Never have I lived with such confidence toward God; never in such intimate union with Jesus; never with such a realization of being seated with Christ in heavenly places. When I yielded up the habit of contemplating sin or expecting myself to sin, I took a great step toward being preserved from it. The new habit of expecting Christ to safely keep me from sin is a wonderful strength to my soul.

Do you think it presumptuous to expect Jesus to save us from sinning? Remember the word: "Thou shalt call his name JESUS: for *he shall save his people from their sins*" (Matt. 1:21, italics added).

TRUSTING FOR EVERYTHING

When we have faith in Christ for any particular thing that commences by an effort, at times a severe one, that faith becomes by continuance a *holy habit* of the soul. When a person experiences a temporary suspension of life, perhaps in extreme illness, the first breaths drawn are a succession of painful efforts; but as full life is restored, breathing again becomes a habit, almost unconsciously continued. In the same manner, soul sickness is the temporary suspension of resurrection life in the believer's soul. Restoration of that life is an effort, a gasping to get the breath of heaven once again; but after that life is restored, it becomes a habit almost unconscious of effort—a habit of inhaling the pure air of the kingdom of God.

Trusting Christ for each privilege that the Holy Spirit opens before us in the Word becomes a holy habit of the soul. Eventually, when any new grace is set before us, the soul instinctively casts itself upon Christ for its accomplishment.

Soon after my conversion, I expressed my despair of ever being such a Christian as Adelaide Newton. I said that such a remarkable life seemed "not for me."

"Not for you?" exclaimed a friend. "Not for you! You may think yourself a very small vessel, but are you full?"

The admonition sank into my soul. Then and there, I asked God for grace that I may never again look upon any privilege designed for all Christians as though it were not for me. By the grace of God, in the fifteen years since, I do not believe I have discerned any gospel blessing offered to all of God's children without being upon my knees about it till, by faith, I obtained it.

When the fuller privileges of sanctification dawned upon me nearly ten years after my conversion, I did not say, "Not for me!" Instead, in the very first moment I apprehended them I claimed them as my own.

With gratitude I remember how gently God taught me the habit of trusting Christ for everything. At first it was a mighty effort to leave *all* to Him. In the emergencies of life, self would seek to assert itself first; and it was subdued at times only after a violent struggle. But in this blessed school of God, I have learned simply and naturally—as the helpless child clings to its parent without first trying its own strength—to habitually trust Jesus in everything. I have learned to be very bold in asking for great things. But when I have made even my largest request, I still find my heavenly Father doing "exceeding abundantly above all that we ask or think" (Eph. 3:20).

IMPLICIT OBEDIENCE

When believers toy with temptation or sin, they scarcely know what they are doing. They should consider not only the dreadful nature of every act of disobedience but the fatal results of interrupting a holy habit of obedience. Oh, that I could reach all children of God—especially those who have entered upon this experience of full soul union with Jesus—and implore them to yield *implicit obedience to every motion of the Spirit of God*; beseech them to do this instantly; and beg them to form the holy habit of perfect obedience! God is so mindful of His own glory and our highest happiness that He will fully manifest himself only to those who give Him their undivided heart, with the result of entire obedience. Every act of disobedience, however small, opens the door for another sin; while every day of consecration gives accumulative force to our future consecration by causing us to gravitate toward God. For years I have known a man whose every emotion, action, and thought has seemed permeated by the presence of God. Recently, he told me the secret of his power, saying that he will soon complete twenty-one years in which *he has kept his obedience at the leading edge of his light.* Such an example of holy manhood may make some of us feel ashamed—not that we should despair, as though such living was not for us, but that it may lead us to claim such precious faith.

As to my own experience, I can glory in nothing save Christ my Lord. But I may say this: After years of my vacillation in obedience, He set before me a path of habitual obedience which, through following His death and resurrection, I have found possible. I now know that the unresisted yoke is easy to bear and the cherished burden is light.

Scripture describes the Holy Spirit in imagery of gentleness—such as the gentle dew or the tender dove—and because I dread to grieve so gentle a monitor, I keep walking softly before God. Saying a hasty word, indulging the spirit of the world, and giving rein to the carnal imagination are things that easily grieve the indwelling Spirit of God! But though the highway of holiness is narrow, God has provided in Jesus an ample means for walking in it. How could I think it presumptuous to trust Jesus to keep me within its limits?

I urge you to form the holy habit of walking in the middle of His highway, as far as possible from the edges, committing yourself in every conscious moment to Jesus. He will keep you out of the ditches that lie on either side of the way.

PRAYER AND SUPPLICATION
WITH THANKSGIVING

The holy habits of prayer and thanksgiving cannot be separated. The apostle Paul tells us, "In every thing by prayer and supplication *with thanksgiving* let your requests be made known unto God. And the peace of God, which passeth all understanding, shall keep your hearts and minds through Christ Jesus" (Phil. 4:6–7, italics added). The peace of God may be compared to a bird, its two wings being prayer and thanksgiving. If either wing fails, the bird must sink. But if, to our believing prayers on the one side, there be joined our expressions of grateful thanks on the other, we "shall mount up with wings as eagles" (Isa. 40:31), and live in the regions of eternal sunshine, far above the malarious damps of the earth.

Most Christians know this as an occasional experience; but how can it become a holy habit of the soul? The question brings us again to the importance of our death to sin and our life unto righteousness, to which our Lord calls us. So long as our body of sin is not destroyed, so long as our faith stumbles at God's promise of inward cleansing from all sin, so long is continuous prayer and thanksgiving impossible. The dead weight of the yet uncrucified carnal nature must sooner or later cause our soul to drop again to the earth.

I encourage every Christian who has realized this wonderful baptism into the death of Christ to walk in newness of life to *"continue* in prayer, and watch in the same with thanksgiving" (Col. 4:2, italics added), to seek patiently from God the attitude of continually turning toward Him. Seek it with your whole heart, for when you seek it in faith, you shall find it.

God has taught me to set before my heart at any given time a single unattained grace, the need of which I feel presented to me in the Word. I must wait upon God for this grace, while watching against every temptation to failure. Sometimes my faith and patience have been tried, but *the end of persevering faith is sure.* Often there has stolen over my heart the realization that my prayer has been answered, and my soul has (almost unconscious of the process) found itself exercising the habit for which it has been praying. In this manner, praise became the natural expression of my heart. Prayer is now not so much the effort as the attitude of my soul. I speak not as one who realizes all that I have claimed of God in these respects; but I do know something of God's power within my soul as I see these holy habits bestowed upon me in answer to prayer and faith.

So gently, so sweetly does our Elder Brother deal with those who put their whole trust in Him! He proves that a thankful heart is a receiving heart.

WITNESSING FOR CHRIST

No one can overestimate the importance of having the holy, continuous habit of witnessing for Christ. Some believers seem to lose no opportunity, day or night, of speaking to sinners about Him; and they seem to win more people by these private labors than most who have many opportunities for public preaching. Their spiritual life flows easily and naturally, like a current of fresh water in its channel. God seems to give a double portion of His Spirit's guidance and power to those who thus zealously use His gifts. While some are fascinated by the gift, these people strive for the increase; while some seek spiritual strength, these people have growing strength by exercise.

I know some people in humble walks of life who might not be welcome in many pulpits; yet, in their own quiet way, they gather hundreds of souls into the kingdom of God. Few know of their work, for the approval of Jesus satisfies their hearts. I have learned many a lesson from such quiet witnesses.

Once I rented a house in a village so that I could preach the gospel in a large tent for those who would not attend church; but with all of my busyness about the public services, I did not take the time to speak to the person in the house next to my own. A very humble brother, who attended the meeting one night and then lodged with me, got up at sunrise and visited with my neighbor as he cultivated his garden. This dear Christian did what I had not done in the weeks I had been there: He warned the neighbor of his soul's peril and invited him to come to Christ. This same man makes it his practice at funerals to select an unconverted person to accompany him to the cemetery, so that he might share the gospel with him. Witnessing for Christ has become the *holy habit* of his life—not a mechanical effort, but a gift that he has diligently improved as he exercises it in the power of God.

The Lord would have those who have received His greatest gifts to be the most diligent laborers for Him. With the gift of righteousness, the cleansed heart, and the indwelling of God, there comes the responsibility of being continuously co-workers with God. He does not expect Spirit-filled believers to make a spasmodic effort of feebleness; He expects a firm, sound march of spiritual health and power. It is not difficult for our mouths to speak out of the abundance that our hearts possess; nevertheless, it is important to form the *holy habit* of speaking on behalf of the Lord. With this habit of speaking of God's grace comes an increase of power. Nothing so raises our feeble longing for full resurrection life as our telling of what Christ has done for our own souls.

In my own case, this habit of speaking to others about my inner life is the reversing of a lifelong education of maintaining entire silence, even toward those nearest to me. I do not remember, in my first ten years of Christian life, to have spoken once about my Christian experience; indeed, I often could not bear to speak of it to anyone but my compassionate Savior! But when it pleased God to fill my soul, I was *compelled* to break the ice of this lifelong habit of silence, so that I had to form the new habit of speaking about what Christ had done for my soul. I shrank at times from it. But a careful study of the Word convinced me that the apostle Paul had shown me the pattern, and that I must by this means reach the souls of sinner and saint. From the addresses of Paul to the unconverted we may deduce that on almost every occasion he opened his ministry to sinners by describing how God had converted his own soul. And from Paul's epistles we may gather that, when he had stated a doctrine, it was his custom to illustrate it by his own experience. For example, when he reproved and warned the Galatians, he opened his own heart and told them, "I do not frustrate the grace of God" (Gal. 2:21). Uncovering the veil of his inner consciousness, he showed them the secret workings of his own life in the words, "Yet not I, but Christ liveth in me: and the life which I now live in the flesh I live by the faith of the Son of God" (v. 20). Matthew Henry says:

What God has *wrought in our souls,* as well as for them, we must declare to others. . . .God's people should communicate their experience to teach others; we should take all occasions to tell how great and kind things God hath done for us, especially our souls, the spiritual blessings; and these we should be most affected with ourselves, and *with these we should endeavor* to affect others.

The commentator Thomas Scott says:

Every servant of God is a witness for Him; and they all can give such an account of what He has wrought in them, shown to them, and done for them, as to lead others to know, believe, and understand His power, truth, and love. . . .I likewise learned the use of experience in preaching, and was convinced that the readiest way to reach the hearts and consciences of others, was to speak from my own.

Bishop Hugh Latimer said of Thomas Bilney's experience, "I learned more by this confession than by much reading, and in many years."

Two marked illustrations of the power of the personal testimony have occurred within a few days. In one case, a prominent and zealous preacher had been unwilling to confess what God had done for him; he thus had failed to enjoy the full privileges of walking in Christ. To his arguments against speaking of his own inner experience, I simply replied, "What most effectively reached you and led you to full sanctification? Was it doctrine and argument, or a Christian friend's confession of what God had wrought in his own soul?"

"I see it. I am all wrong," was the frank reply. "It was someone's personal experience that reached my heart. I am now ready to acknowledge all that Christ shall do for me."

Again, for some weeks I had been holding a series of meetings in the farmhouses near my summer home, but without any manifest results. There was deep interest and the attendance was good, but no one acknowledged being saved. After a time, I was led by the Spirit to tell at the close of a meeting what God had done *for me*. That night there was one clear conversion. At the next meeting, eight or ten persons made confession of having been saved during or immediately after the meeting. I trace this remarkable work to the power of God, which accompanied my confession of His past and present grace in my life.

When, like Paul, the preacher comes to the point of telling about God's dealings with his own soul, all eyes and hearts are fixed upon him and a personal interest is awakened. Successful evangelists find that their own narrative of God's grace in their lives is the most effective arrow for reaching the hearts of the King's enemies. Therefore, should not our sharing of God's further dealings with our souls be as effective toward the friends of Christ, in calling them to allow God's full power to reign within their souls? When one gives Christ all the glory for His work, I do not believe that one narrative savors of presumption any more than the other.

After prayer and careful searching of the Word of God, several Christians have made allusions to their personal experiences in print. I suppose that no portion of the literature on Christian sanctification has so touched the hearts of the saints as have these personal confessions. So it is with deep conviction that I press upon you the habit of personally relating, under proper circumstances, God's gracious dealings with you. The abuse of such a practice must not deter you from its use, any more than a hundred other perversions that might be named. Satan, who knows the power of such a testimony, would raise a thousand objections. To him we give one sufficient reply—the example of the saints in all ages, guided by the Holy Spirit, as related in the Word of God.

Our Lord himself, our pattern in this as in all else, has opened His heart to us in the Psalms. He has been followed in this by the prophets and the apostles, men "subject to like passions as we are" (James 5:17), who have taught us in many a heart-searching personal lesson what could not have been so effectively taught otherwise.

"Come and hear, all ye that fear God, and I will declare what he hath done for my soul" (Ps. 66:16).

"The LORD hath done great things for us; whereof we are glad" (Ps. 126:3).

"Ye are witnesses, and God also, how holily and justly and unblamably we behaved ourselves among you that believe" (1 Thess. 2:10).

"For our rejoicing is this, the testimony of our conscience, that in simplicity and godly sincerity, not with fleshly wisdom, but by the grace of God, we have had our conversation in the world, and more abundantly to you-ward" (2 Cor. 1:12).

May the Lord increase this holy habit of witnessing of His grace! Though some may misunderstand us, "the humble shall hear thereof, and be glad" (Ps. 34:2). Many shall be roused to know the fullness of God's grace when we testify, "Thou hast delivered my soul from death, mine eyes from tears, and my feet from falling" (Ps. 116:8).

THE
CHRISTIAN'S SHOUT

THE CHRISTIAN'S SHOUT

By Hannah Whitall Smith

HERE is a scene in the history of the children of Israel that reveals in type one of the precious secrets of the Lord which are progressively made known to those who love Him. And perhaps there is no revelation made to the soul, after it has entered upon the life of faith, that is more practically valuable than this. For it is a secret that, when it is discovered, makes the Christian's warfare a long triumphal progress.

We find this scene when the children of Israel were brought before Jericho, one of those "cities. . . great, and walled up to heaven" (Deut. 1:28), which had so discouraged the hearts of their spies forty years before. Now upon their entrance into the Promised Land, the first difficulty that met them was this mighty city. Well might their hearts have been appalled at the sight of it. But the Lord said to Joshua, "See, I have given into thine hand Jericho, and the king thereof, and the mighty men of valor"(Josh. 6:2). After a few words as to their order of march and the trumpets of testimony, the Lord closed His instructions with these strange words: "All the people shall shout with a great shout; and the wall of the city shall fall down flat, and the people shall ascend up every man straight before him" (v. 5). So the people shouted when the priests blew the trumpets. "And it came to pass, when the people heard the sound of the trumpet, and the people shouted with a great shout, that the wall fell down flat, so that the people went up into the city, every man straight before him, *and they took the city*" (v. 20b, italics added).

Now no one can suppose for a moment that the Israelites' shout caused the walls to fall. Yet the secret of their victory lay in their shout, for it was the shout of faith that dared to claim a promised victory, on the authority of God's word alone, before there was any sign of its being accomplished. According to their faith, God did unto them; when *they* shouted *He* made the walls to fall.

God declared that He had given them the city, and their faith reckoned this to be true. Unbelief might well have said, "It would be better not to shout until the walls actually fall, lest we bring dishonor to the name of our God." But faith laughed at such prudential considerations and, confidently resting on God's word, gave a shout of victory while the victory seemed impossible. Long centuries afterward, the Holy Spirit recorded this triumph of faith in Hebrews 11:30: "By faith the walls of Jericho fell down, after they were compassed about seven days."

Jehoshaphat was another example of this sort of faith. Second Chronicles 20:2 reports that a "great multitude" had come up against him. But he spread the case before the Lord and received as an answer the wonderful promise, "Ye shall not need to fight in this battle: set yourselves, stand ye still, and see the salvation of the LORD with you, O Judah and Jerusalem: fear not, nor be dismayed; tomorrow go out against them: for the LORD will be with you" (v. 17). Jehoshaphat believed what God said, so he and his people marched out to meet their enemy, as confident of victory as though they had seen it already accomplished before their eyes. They even appointed singers to praise the Lord and to sing the song of victory as they went out to meet their foe. And we read that "when they began to sing and to praise, the LORD set ambushments against [the enemy]; and they were smitten" (v. 22). When the Israelites came near them, "they looked unto the multitude, and, behold, they were dead bodies fallen to the earth, and none escaped" (v. 24). Truly more than conquerors, "they were three days in gathering of the spoil, it was so much" (v. 25).

The principle of warfare depicted in this account is also declared in 1 John 5:4: "And this is the victory that overcometh the world, even our faith." It is a mode of warfare incomprehensible to the natural man; a mystery even to the Christian whose faith has not advanced beyond the failing experience of Romans 7; but it is radiant with the light of the Holy Spirit to every soul that has entered upon the life hidden with Christ in God. Only such a person can understand the full meaning of our Lord when He said, "Be of good cheer; I have overcome the world" (John 16:33). In this declaration we find the secret of an already conquered foe. Knowing this secret, we can go out to meet our enemies, claiming the victory before the battle has even begun. So in truth we can become "more than conquerors through him that loved us" (Rom. 8:37).

Observe that Joshua did not say, "Shout; for the Lord *will give* you the city." He said, "Shout; for the LORD *hath given* you the city" (Josh. 6:16, italics added). And neither did our Lord say, "Be of good cheer; I *will overcome* the world." He said, "I *have overcome* the world." There is a great difference between these two understandings—as great a difference as there is between meeting an army in full battle array or meeting one that is routed and demoralized because it already acknowledges its defeat. So long as an army can keep secret the fact of its being conquered, it can still make some show of resistance. But the moment its defeat is known, the army loses heart and becomes utterly demoralized. It has no choice but to flee.

The secret then lies in this: to consider our enemy an already conquered foe, and not as one yet to be conquered. It is the one secret that Satan seeks to hide from the church, and in doing this he has only too well succeeded. A dear Christian, who had been fearfully beset by temptation and had found a complete victory nearly impossible, was told this secret by another to whom it had been revealed. Her soul rejoiced in the discovery. She said afterward that it seemed as though she could almost hear Satan exclaiming, "There! She has found out my secret! She knows now that I am already conquered, and so I shall never have any more victories over her."

Surely it is true that Jesus has fought our enemy and overcome him. And if only our faith will reckon him to be overcome—if it will dare to raise the shout of victory when it comes in sight of any foe—we shall surely find, as the Israelites did, that every wall will fall down flat. A pathway will be opened up before us to take the city!

And now a few practical words about *how* to do this. Our usual way of meeting temptation is to raise a cry of help. We say, "O Lord, save me!" Let us meet it hereafter with a shout of victory instead. Let us say by faith, "He *does* save me." The walls may look as high and as immovable as ever; prudence may say that it is not safe to shout until they have fallen. But faith that can shout in the midst of temptation, "Jesus saves me *now*!" will be sure to win a glorious and speedy victory. I have often tried this. Temptations have poured in like a flood—temptations to be irritable, to think wicked thoughts, to become bitter in spirit, or to do a thousand other things. I have felt the imminent danger of sinning, and my fears have said that Jesus will not save me from it. But then my faith has exclaimed, "Jesus saves me—saves me *now*!" And the deliverance was glorious. Sometimes it seemed so untrue that Jesus could save me that I have had to say aloud, "He does save." I have forced my lips to utter it over and over, shutting my eyes and closing my ears to every suggestion of the Devil to doubt. Untrue though it seemed at first, I have always found that when I shouted the victory, the Lord never failed to give it to me.

A Christian trolley car man, who had a naturally harsh temper, had entered upon this life of faith but was sorely beset with temptations when he was about his daily work among his ungodly companions. One morning on his way to his trolley stand, he stopped at the house of the minister who had led him into this blessed experience, in order to ask how he could best meet and conquer these temptations. After explaining how they suddenly presented themselves, so that he seldom had time even to pray for help against them, the car man said, "Now can you tell me of any short road to victory, a help that I can lay hold of at just the needed moment?"

"Yes," replied the minister. "When temptation comes, do not stop to pray for help. Instead, claim by faith the promised victory, and Satan will instantly flee."

The car man went on his way. As usual, he was met by the taunts of his fellow workers. He soon found that they had jostled him out of his rightful place in the ranks of the trolley cars; in fact, they had pushed him to the end of the line. He was greatly tempted to be angry. But, folding his arms, he said at once, "The blood of Jesus cleanseth me!" And his heart was filled again with perfect peace and contentment. Again he was tried when a heavy box was rolled so as to fall on his foot and hurt him. Again he folded his arms and repeated his shout of victory, and all was calm. And so the day passed. Trials and temptations abounded, but his triumphal shout carried him safely through them all, and the fiery darts of the Enemy were deflected by the shield of faith that he continually lifted up. Nighttime found him more than a conqueror through Him who loved him, and his fellow car men were forced to see the beauty of a religion that could triumph over aggravating assaults.

Dear Christian, try this. Go out to meet your enemy, singing a song of triumph as you go, and I promise you on the authority of God's Word that your faith shall be rewarded. Meet your very next temptation this way. At its first approach, begin to give thanks for the victory you have over it, and you will find such triumph as you have heretofore scarcely imagined.

FAILURE

FAILURE

N THIS life of faith, as we have repeatedly stated, there is no necessity for failure. We affirm that there are resources available to the believer—in the cleansing blood of Christ, in the sanctifying Word of God, and in the indwelling Holy Spirit—ample to preserve anyone from all consciousness of transgression. We find that to "walk in the Spirit," to "dwell in love," and to know the Father and Son making their "abode" with us is not merely a distant hope but a present reality. But we have never said that there is no longer any possibility of our sinning. We have rather most earnestly exhorted and urged all Christians to see that they should strive to continually abide in Christ, lest they again be brought "into captivity to the law of sin" (Rom. 7:23), from which they have through faith found deliverance.

However, some who have commenced to "walk in the light" seem enabled to press on in one continuous and unvarying life of triumph, while others' experiences are not so unwavering. The latter have entered upon the highway of holiness and know that they are walking therein almost continuously; but now and then they are suddenly surprised into a momentary lapse, so that they fall into some easily besetting sin. The questions at once arise: How does this affect their Christian experience? What are they to do? Shall they lose all heart to trust the keeping power of Christ? Shall they turn back to the Christ-dishonoring attitudes of the past, never again going to Jesus for full deliverance?

Shall remembrance of their failure remain as a canker in their breasts, destroying all hope of victory? Because they have supposed there is absolutely no failure in the lives of others who testify of the rest of faith, shall they cross their Jordan again, to resume a wilderness experience of failure and defeat?

Notice that right between the two passages of Scripture that so absolutely declare the promise of the believer's inward cleansing "from all sin" and "from all unrighteousness" we find a warning against any claim to inherent righteousness, any goodness in ourselves apart from the purifying blood of Christ. We also find the provision, in case of failure, for God's instantaneous pardon upon the confession of our sin. The passage reads thus:

> But if we walk in the light, as he is in the light, we have fellowship one with another, and the blood of Jesus Christ his Son cleanseth us from all sin. If we say that we have no sin, we deceive ourselves, and the truth is not in us. If we confess our sins, he is faithful and just to forgive us our sins, and to cleanse us from all unrighteousness (1 John 1:7–9).

The promise of pardon is this: After we have known divine fellowship in the light of God and have been inwardly cleansed from all sin, should there be a revival of old evil in our hearts with consequent trespass against God, *the same instant* in which we become conscious of our sin we should make its free and full confession. Simultaneous with the conviction of trespass and its confession, the soul should realize that God is faithful to His promise and has forgiven the sin. The penalty that Christ has borne for us "in his own body on the cross" (1 Peter 2:24, para.), is not to be endured a second time by us.

Nor does God's blessed promise stop here. It carries us onward to the inward recleansing of the heart "from all unrighteousness," from the internal taint caused by our lapse of faith that preceded the trespass. Thus, the same flash of consciousness shall realize the sin. . .the confession. . .the forgiveness. . .and the soul cleansing in a single instant of time. So instantaneous a use of God's provision for pardon will restore the soul at once to the keeping power of Christ. Those who have learned to avail themselves of this immediate resumption of their heavenly privilege know how tender, trustful, and victorious the restored communion with God can be.

Allow me to share an instance from my own experience. Many years ago I learned faith's secret of hourly victory over my enemies. Christ became my shield, and I learned to so place that shield between temptation and my soul that, hour by hour and day by day, I found myself overcoming temptation where I had before been sure to fail. I found rest instead of a troubled, self-condemning heart. I wondered at this inward Sabbath of my soul; indeed, I may have wondered at it so much that I lost the full realization of how exclusively it was Christ's victory and rest, not my own. One day a workman had disarranged my plans and so perplexed me that my naturally hasty temper ignited like a flash of powder. Instead of turning first to Christ, I stepped up to the workman and reproved him in a harsh tone of voice. Immediately came the consciousness that I had sinned. Two courses of action were then open to me: One was to allow my consciousness of sinning to separate me from the presence of Jesus, thus bringing gloom and consequent failure. The other and better way was to let *the very first moment* of this consciousness bring me to confession and perfect pardon, as well as inward cleansing from the evil that gave rise to the hasty words I had spoken. Having done this, my rest of soul was at once restored. Instead of allowing the circumstance to keep me from the heart of Jesus, I was humbled and more conscious of my dependence upon Him. Instead of remaining separated from Christ and therefore vulnerable to the wiles of Satan, I again found my place "in Christ" and was strengthened against a recurrence of the sin.

(I might add that my immediate acknowledgment of my hasty speech made a deep impression on the workman. The wrong and the prompt apology became a testimony of the power of God in my soul, rather than a stumbling block in his own way. Shortly afterward, I had the joy of leading him to a public confession of Christ in a Presbyterian church service.)

Human beings reverse God's plan, from His first teaching of law to the sinner to His latest instructions to the saint. "To be good is to be happy," so many of us suppose. But in the life of grace the rule should rather read, "To be happy is to be good." That is to say, the soul that is joyful in Jesus and allows no cloud to shut out the rays of the Sun of Righteousness is strong to overcome, to work, or to suffer for Christ. Let us *become* right in order to do right, rather than *do* in order to become. God's first expression of love to the sinner is to make him joyful in the knowledge of forgiven sin, so that the joy of the Lord becomes the source of his new strength. Surely He acts in no less grace toward the saint!

The Christian who lives thus is like a ship heading directly toward its port. Even if a sudden wave strikes its side, throwing it "on its beam ends," it is instantly righted and continues on its course. The needle of its compass may be for a moment deflected; but when the deflecting cause is removed, it reverts at once to its normal direction.

Those who have learned to trust the power of Jesus must give up the expectation of sinning. Should sin occur, it must be their painful surprise, not their expectation. They will surely find as they walk in Christ that even such occasional failures begin to fade from their experience. Should sin occur, they fly instantly back to Jesus, since their heavenly Father has promised, "Thy sins and thine iniquities I will remember no more" (Heb. 10:17, para.), They feel it their privilege also to forget the failures forever, so that again they may know the reality of the promise, "The LORD upholdeth all that fall" (Ps. 145:14).

However, if failure becomes more rather than less frequent in the believer's life, there is a radical defect in his consecration and faith. Let such a one cry, "Search me, O God, and know my heart: try me, and know my thoughts: and see if there be any wicked way in me, and lead me in the way everlasting" (Ps. 139:23–24). The light of God's truth will discover the hidden cause of failure; and what the searching light reveals, the precious blood of Christ will cleanse.

Let no earnest Christian be discouraged to feel that the consciousness of sin is more painful than ever before. Rather let him give thanks that his conscience has become tender. The more a Christian walks in Christ, the greater will be his hatred of sin. The psalmist says of Christ, "Thou lovest righteousness, and *hatest* wickedness: therefore God, thy God, hath anointed thee with the oil of gladness above thy fellows" (Ps. 45:7, italics added). The often-wounded conscience becomes insensitive to sin, while the "conscience void of offense" (Acts 24:16), becomes tender.

Let us beware of one special snare of Satan—that of trying to persuade us that temptation or mere infirmity is sin. Christ was "in all points tempted like as we are, yet without sin" (Heb. 4:15). His temptations were actual; His pressures to do evil were real. Yet He yielded not, so was without sin. Neither is the unwelcomed, unindulged, rejected temptation a sin to us.

Of many things, such as physical incapacity for continued earnest attention to duties before us, we may safely say, "This is my infirmity." We need not allow Satan to condemn us on this account. At our best, however, we must daily cry, "Forgive us our trespasses." Everything in and about us is imperfect, and we need every moment the merit of the blood of Christ.

Someone may ask, "If then you have found failure and condemnation at times in this life of faith, wherein does it differ from your previous experience of conscious pardon and constant failure?"

It differs as a book of white paper, in which one

finds on the first pages some signs of erased errors, differs from a book with scribblings on every page. It differs as the march of Cromwell's army, assured of victory, differed from that of the discouraged royalists. It differs as a clear day on the peak of Mont Blanc differs from the cloudy day in the valley below.

A Presbyterian elder once told me that the most exhilarating day of his life was passed on the heights of a mountain in Switzerland. His guide, notwithstanding a heavy rainstorm, had advised his party to make the ascent, promising that they would find clear sunshine above the clouds. Some of the party believed the guide, ascended the mountain, and found a magnificent view of an almost cloudless sky. The rest of the group, not believing him, remained in the valley beneath the clouds. After a day of intense enjoyment, my friend descended to the hotel and found the others watching the rain beat against the windows. So it had been, he said, with his own soul. Then he believed the word of his trusted Christian friends, he trusted Jesus, and he entered a level of faith that was to his soul "above the clouds." After thirty years of being silent in prayer meetings, his tongue was loosed to praise God and tell out of a full heart what it is to "walk in the light."

The better life that we seek to portray differs from the former Christian life as Romans 6 and 8 differ from Romans 7. It differs as a life characterized by abiding in Christ differs from one that frequently loses communion with Him. It differs as a healthy tree, which is ever-expanding in every direction, differs from one plagued by inward decay and weakness. The two may seem quite similar at first in their outward appearance; the weak may even seem fairer to look upon, but the other has the full power of life.

Oh, for this power to live more abundantly in all of those who believe on Christ!

I seek to encourage honest souls who have fully consecrated themselves to God, renounced their own wills, and trusted unreservedly in the promises of God—people who yet feel they have not been invariably kept from sin. God forbid that we should open any door for the expectation of sinning. Often it is a test of our faith, whether we will continue to live as other people do, or so cast ourselves upon the promises of God as to give up the expectation of sinning. Nothing short of claiming those promises is full faith in Jesus.

We must yield up the unbelief that says, "I shall someday fall by the hand of my enemies." We must instead say, "I can do all things through Christ." That is to grasp the victory of faith. There is a wide difference between stumbling as a sudden and painful surprise (which is the experience of the most consecrated believer) and expecting to continue in sin (which is the gloomy outlook of one without faith).

Happy is the Christian who, walking in the light, does not stumble. Happy too is the one who, when suddenly overtaken in a fault, finds that the failure need not lead to other missteps, but realizes that an instantaneous restoration makes the failure a means of future victory in the very direction in which the trespass has occurred.

LOVE:
THE BOND OF
PERFECTNESS

LOVE:
THE BOND OF PERFECTNESS

HERE are some who feel that by faith they have found victory over the world, the flesh, and the Devil, yet feel that something is lacking in their Christian experience. They run well the race of life for a time; they seem filled with the presence and power of Christ; and so far as they can tell, they are "dead" to the world and their life is "hid with Christ in God" (Col. 3:3). And yet—there is a *yet* remaining—they find at times they are suddenly jostled by the old evil nature that springs up again. So long as their life went calmly, they were like a jar of clear water through which the rays of the sun might shine. But under sudden disturbance, they are like the same jar when it has been shaken, and its sediment stirred up once again, making the water cloudy and incapable of transmitting the sun's rays. After all, the sediment has remained, though for a time it was not apparent. So they are disheartened and exclaim, "Is there no remedy for this? Cannot the Christ who saves me also *keep* me from being overcome by these sudden assaults of temptation?"

They have tried to watch against temptation. But in the fleeting moment when their perseverance has relaxed, the assault comes. They cannot make vows to God anymore, for they have learned too well that they are unable to fulfill them. Clinging to Christ becomes at times a painful effort.* And they feel that abiding within the citadel of faith, where they would be "kept by the power of God," is a privilege beyond their reach. Even their prayers seem at times to lack the faith that makes them effectual. These weary seekers are brought to that point of despair where, at the end of all the resources they know, they are ready to learn any new lesson that the Holy Spirit might teach them in the Word. This lesson may be found at the end of the New Testament's list of Christian graces: "And above all these things put on charity [love], which is the bond of perfectness. And let the peace of God rule in your hearts, to the which also ye are called in one body; and be ye thankful" (Col. 3:14–15). Having received the graces of the Spirit, they yet need something to bind those graces together and keep them in harmonious proportion. Love will do this; it is "the bond of

---

*A popular painting represents a young woman clinging in desperation to a rough stone cross, while sea waves surge all around, about to engulf her. This indeed represents the attitude of one who has just come to Christ. But if I were the artist, I would paint another scene: The cross upon an eternal rock, in the midst of green pastures and still waters, with a refreshed pilgrim resting peacefully beneath its shadow, yet gazing with tear-filled eyes over the perishing mariners in the distance. Such a figure would display the restfulness of imparted strength, but would have the attitude of moving toward their rescue. Likewise, it is now in our power to cling unceasingly to the Cross. We have our feet set upon a rock, with the everlasting arms of God supporting us.

perfectness." Love gives harmony and power to all else that we receive from the Spirit. If we keep ourselves "in the love of God," all other graces that we receive from Him will thrive. Faith and hope shall one day give place to sight; but love is the present and eternal condition of the redeemed who overcome all evil. "Love never faileth" (1 Cor 13:8, para.).

It would seem very bold to claim of God a love that "suffereth long and is kind," "envieth not," "vaunteth not itself," "is not puffed up" (1 Cor. 13:4)—a love that answers injury and reproach with a sweetness that is without effort, simply expressing the undisturbed interior calm of the soul. It would seem still more bold to ask of God this love as the unfailing garrison of the soul, protecting it from all assaults, however unexpected or sudden. When memory recalls all of our past failures, or when our sight surveys the innumerable perplexities and vexations of life that form the momentary enemies to godly love, well might we exclaim, "Impossible!" But here, as elsewhere in our Christian experience, faith negates the verdict of sight and sense to cry, "It shall be done!" At every stage of our onward progress, we are called to put our trust in "God, who quickeneth the dead, and calleth those things which be not as though they were" (Rom. 4:17). We are summoned to be like Abraham, who "staggered not at the promise of God through unbelief; but was strong in faith, giving glory to God; and being fully persuaded that, what he had promised, he was able also to perform" (vv. 20–21). This is the faith that brings God onto the scene, the faith that calls forth this blessing of God's divine love abiding in us.

We have less difficulty in realizing that this perfected trust and its accompanying perfect love is now for us when we remember that it is not our own natural love, the emotions proceeding from our own soul, that constitute "the love of God." Nor is "the peace of God" our soul's peaceful attitude toward God; it is His eternal peace, which He sends down into the hearts of His trusting children. Likewise, the love of God is born not "of the will of the flesh, nor of the will of man, but of God" (John 1:13). It is a divine gift, like the Holy Spirit, by whom it "is shed abroad in our hearts" (Rom. 5:5). The love of God is not a condition of the soul into which we can gradually grow, but a divine grace bestowed upon the trusting heart.

Since this love is of God, it is perfect in its character, free and immediate in its bestowal, and (through our continuing faith and obedience) permanent in its results. And since it answers our soul's deepest need, *now* is the time we should receive it. I do not see how any believer need despair of having the full power of the love of God, since it is to be received as a gift from God, undeserved but freely bestowed.

Once we have received the love of God, we have the responsibility of keeping ourselves in it. Yesterday's building seems today as but a foundation that was laid, so that we are continually called to build further upon it.

Oh, that God's love in all its fullness might be received by all who have lived too long in the changing atmosphere of their natural emotions! Oh, that you would abandon yourself to this love of Jesus Christ until you could say, "He brought me to the banqueting house, and his banner over me was love" (Song of Sol. 2:4)! There are some believers whose very hearts melt within them as they experience this divinely begotten love of God.

Only our full acceptance of this love can satisfy the desires of our heavenly Bridegroom, who tells us that His "love is strong as death. . . . Many waters cannot quench love, neither can the floods drown it: if a man would give all the substance of his house for love, it would utterly be contemned" (Song of Sol. 8:6–7).

Thank God if you feel the need of this overcoming divine love, even if you nearly despair of experiencing it. The felt need of a grace promised in God's Word is the first step toward His supplying of your need. Lay your need before God. Hide His Word in your heart. Do not go away and forget your need amid the many competing voices in the world and in your heart, but keep it as your soul's cry, continually before His throne. Can you doubt what the result will be?

Do not be discouraged if you have not yet been "made perfect in love." Remember that the apostle Peter spoke of "the *ornament* of a meek and quiet spirit" (1 Pet. 3:4, italics added). In building a house, we do not put ornaments on the facade until a strong foundation has been laid and the walls erected. Likewise, we are first "rooted and built up in him, and stablished in the faith" (Col. 2:17), and *then* the diadem of divine love is placed upon us. To the beholder, the ornaments are the most conspicuous and most beautiful parts of the house; but to the home dweller, the secure foundation and walls are most important. Remember that the Lord who erects "God's temple" will assuredly complete it, so that He himself shall dwell there evermore.

I realize that I am incapable of conveying the inward sense of these things. Yet I find comfort in quoting these words of one who dwelt in the love of God about two centuries ago, and whose testimony still lives:

What is Love? What shall I say of it, or how shall I in words express its nature? It is the sweetness of life; it is the sweet, tender, melting nature of God, flowing up through His seed of life into the creature, and of all things making the creature most like himself, both in nature and operation. It fulfills the law, it fulfills the gospel; it wraps up all in one, and brings forth all in the oneness. It excludes all evil out of the heart, it perfects all good in the heart. A touch of this love doth this in measure; perfect love does this in fullness. . . .

And this my soul waits and cries after, . . . that the life of God in its own perfect sweetness may fully run forth through this vessel, and not be at all tinctured by the vessel, but perfectly tincture and change the vessel into its own nature. . . .

Here is found a genuine humility which, while it acknowledges God's work in forgiveness, in victory over sin, in cleansing, and in the divine gift of all-pervading love, recognizes the duty of the soul to facilitate and continue God's work. Saint Augustine said, "As when we load a vessel, the more ballast we put in, the lower it sinks; so the more love we have in the soul, the lower we are abased in self. The side of the scale which is elevated is empty; so the soul is elated when it is void of love."

Let us so charge ourselves with the weight of love as to bring self down to its just level. Let its depths be manifested by our readiness to bear the humiliations and the sufferings that are necessary to the purification of the soul. Our humiliation is our exaltation. "Whosoever is least among you shall be the greatest" (Luke 9:48, para.), says the Lord. Let us die to all but God.

SUFFERING
WITH CHRIST

SUFFERING
WITH CHRIST

WE HAVE many who love us, many who share our hours of joy, many to whom we may tell our past enjoyments or future hopes. But few are those to whom we open the sorrows of our hearts or the inward agonies of our souls. We must sense a very unusual knitting of their hearts to ours—a deep conviction that they will sympathize with our grief—before we can open to them the secrets of our lives. And when those recesses of our souls have been exposed to another human being, that person will thenceforth have a sacred nearness to us, beyond any other person's fellowship in our joys, hopes, or labors. We will feel a wonderful bond with that person, woven by a sorrow suffered by one and experienced over again, through sympathy, by the other. While it may be easy to separate those who have only enjoyed or labored together, it will take much to alienate those who have suffered together. The sacred bond of common grief binds two people more closely together than anything else in life.

Let us apply this observation to our relationship with the Lord. "Henceforth I call you not servants; . . . I have called you *friends*," our Lord says in John 15:15 (italics added). He has friends to whom He unfolds what He is about to do. He has friends who share the righteousness, the peace, and the joy that belong to His kingdom. He has friends whom He sends forth, endued with the mighty power of His Spirit, to win souls to himself. He has friends whose ear He arouses morning by morning to hear His voice, so that they may speak to those who are weary, teaching and building them up in their most holy faith. Yet there is a higher privilege than even these callings of divine friendship—a privilege that few believers understand, and even fewer are willing to accept—the privilege of knowing His fellowship in *suffering*.

When Saul of Tarsus, the greatest of Christ's messengers, was called to work for the Master, Jesus said, "I will show him how great things he must *suffer* for my name's sake" (Acts 9:16, italics added). Afterward Paul had to say, "The sufferings of Christ abound in us" (2 Cor. 1:5). Paul trod in Christ's footsteps. Christ suffered, and so did Paul; Jesus wept over Jerusalem, and so did Paul weep over those who were still enemies to the Cross; Jesus was moved by the attitude of the Jews, being "grieved for the hardness of their hearts" (Mark 3:5), and Paul travailed until Christ should be formed in the Judaizing Christians. Of Jesus the Jews said, "Away with him, away with him, crucify him" (John 19:15). And of Paul they said, "Away with such a fellow from the earth: for it is not fit that he should live" (Acts 22:22).

Many people aspire to having intimate, peaceful communion with Christ; but few want to commune with Him in the more sacred experience of suffering. Many seek the joys of salvation, but few are ready to fill up that which remains of the afflictions of Christ for the sake of His church.

Few people have recognized the privileges of the dispensation in which God has placed them. For forty years, the Israelites preferred the wilderness to the Promised Land. While living under the immediate rule of God, they sought to crown a king. John the Baptist, although mightily used by the Holy Spirit to proclaim Jesus as the Messiah of Israel, afterward failed to understand the reason for his humiliation and so sent his disciples to inquire whether Jesus was indeed the Christ. Neither the devout Jews nor the apostles themselves understood until the Day of Pentecost that the Jewish dispensation of law was to be replaced by a dispensation of grace. The Galatians, even after beginning to live in the Spirit, returned to legal bondage, as have most Christians at some stage of their experience. The Corinthians, little understanding the relation of the world to the church, wanted to enjoy their privileges while Paul suffered hunger, thirst, and every privation. So Paul wrote them, "Now ye are full, now ye are rich, ye have reigned as kings without us" (1 Cor. 4:8). He referred not so much to the outward circumstances of Christians, which in the providence of God may greatly vary, but to the inward character of their lives; for a rich man may be poor in spirit, while the poor man may be unduly exalted.

It is so even now. Forgetting that the Heir of the Father has been cast out and that He will soon come again, professing Christians are seeking the glory of this world.

What is it to suffer with Christ, as the peculiar joy

of intimate fellowship with Him, to which we are invited in this dispensation? Scripture says, "If so be that we suffer with him, that we may be also glorified together" (Rom. 8:17); what does that mean? Surely the suffering mentioned here is not the ordained consequence of our own follies or sins. This sort of suffering is common to all people, for it is not to unconverted sinners alone that the warning applies: "He that soweth to his flesh shall of the flesh reap corruption" (Gal. 6:8). Nor does the promise refer to the usual sorrows of humanity, for Christians have the sting extracted from the inevitable sufferings of this life on account of their eternal hope, and in this regard they suffer less than others do. Rather I believe that the promise of Romans 8:17 refers to three kinds of suffering:

1. Suffering persecution for Christ's sake,
2. Suffering the sorrow of Christ over the church, when she is adulterously united with the world, and
3. Fellowship in the grief of Christ over those who reject His salvation.

Let us consider the consequences of sharing each of these three kinds of suffering with our Lord Jesus.

SUFFERING PERSECUTION

Sometimes a Christian will say, "I do not suffer persecution. Hasn't persecution ceased to be the Christian's experience?" But the promise of Scripture is clear: "Yea, and *all* that will live godly in Christ Jesus shall suffer persecution" (2 Tim. 3:12, italics added). Many believers escape persecution on earth and will be found in heaven at last—saved, yet as though they have passed through fire. But those who live "godly in

Christ Jesus" cannot fail but to receive their share of
persecution here and now. Such believers will be
censured for the way they live (alas, censured more
often by those who profess to be Christians than by the
world outside!) Their lives are so hidden with Christ
that few will understand them. They seem alone
because they are so constantly with Jesus. Material
prosperity does not exalt them, nor sorrow depress
them. Having Christ, they are well-satisfied with
whatever may befall them. Crucified to the world, they
are no longer of it. How often, since the martyrdom of
Stephen, have we seen believers whose lives proved
that "the spirit of glory and of God" (1 Peter 4:14),
rested on them when persecution arose? It is a blessed
thing to be "counted worthy to suffer shame for his
name" (Acts 5:41). It is a victorious experience to arm
ourselves with the mind that was in Christ, who
suffered for us in the flesh—knowing that, in proportion to our living in Christ here, we shall share the
distribution of His heavenly rewards in eternity.

SORROW FOR THE CHURCH

As we noted earlier, Paul placed his feet in the
footprints of Jesus; he rejoiced as Jesus rejoiced and
wept as Jesus wept. He served the Ephesians "with
many tears" (Acts 20:19). He wrote to the Corinthians
"with many tears" to warn them of their failures
(2 Cor. 2:4). When he spoke of the enemies of the
gospel among the Philippians, he did so "even weep-
ing" (Phil. 3:18). His was not a mere human sympathy,
but a divinely begotten sorrow. The sufferings of
Christ "abounded" in him, and this affliction resulted
in the "consolation and salvation" of Christ's church.

How I cherish the memory of a loving Christian brother, whose sorrow over the condition of the church seemed to know no bounds. When I learned that he had not slept for several nights in succession, I asked him for the cause. With some reluctance, he replied that the corruptions of the church of God so weighed upon his heart that he was unable to sleep. Like the mourning prophet Jeremiah, he wept and interceded for the people of God through the night. Years afterward, when he died while upon his knees in prayer, I felt his ministry of suffering with Jesus gave him a relationship of peculiar nearness to the Man of Sorrows.

Perhaps you now sense Jesus saying to your heart, "Can *you* drink of the cup that I drink of, and be baptized with the baptism I am baptized with?" (Mark 10:39). Are you willing to be so aware of the sinfulness of the world that you would exclaim, "Oh that my head were waters, and mine eyes a fountain of tears, that I might weep day and night for the slain of the daughter of my people!" (Jer. 9:1)? When a Christian is willing to undergo such experiences of suffering with Christ, he comes forth from the prayer closet endued with the gentleness of Christ, to stir the hearts of those who have lost their love for the Lord and kindle the flame of his own soul within theirs. Such experiences lead us into the very heart of Christ to an extent that is impossible when we share His joy or labor alone.

SORROW FOR THE WORLD

The foundations of Christianity were laid in suffering, and they who drink most deeply of its spirit must share the sufferings of its divine Founder—not in the sense of sharing His atonement, but as all intercessors must suffer for the lost, entering their condition in spirit so that they may lift them up to God.

When greedy ship owners made the voyage to Australia almost like the passage of African slaves, one devoted man decided to relieve the fearful suffering of the emigrants. His first act was to sign aboard the steerage and experience a passage to Australia among them. This must be the attitude of every Christian who intercedes for a dying world.

The tender spirit that is centered in Christ will be, as the poet said, "At leisure from itself, / To soothe and sympathize." Such a person will be baptized into the condition of those for whom he prays and labors, so that he can effectually reach souls whose state has been by sympathy his own. Some Christians know what it is to agonize for sinful people with a sorrow far greater than any personal grief for material loss or bereavement. The Lord seeks such laborers for the work of His harvest.

There is, then, a close correspondence between our close following of Christ here and our eternal position in His kingdom. The small end of the lever, moved by faithfulness here, sweeps the long arm in the heavens for all eternity. But of all the rewards of God's grace to His blood-bought children, none shall bring us so near to Jesus as our fellowship in His sufferings in a day of general failure. "If so be that we suffer *with him*, that we may be also glorified together" (Rom. 8:17, italics added). Though we pray for joy, we find our hearts asking for the opportunity to share the sufferings of Christ for the sake of His church. Our Lord now invites His faithful disciples to this divine fellowship in suffering, this sacred nearness to the suffering Savior.

We do not have to wait for another dispensation to

begin rejoicing in our sufferings, however. There is already a deep joy in suffering, when it is endured for Christ. In proportion "as the sufferings of Christ abound in us, so our consolation also aboundeth by Christ" (2 Cor. 1:5). Undoubtedly, Paul and Silas keenly felt their privation in the stocks as they sat in the inner prison; but a joy welled up in their souls which led them to sing praises to their Lord. Jesus himself was "despised and rejected of men" (Isa. 53:3), yet in the midst of all His persecutions He "rejoiced in spirit" (Luke 10:21), as He saw the deep things of God revealed to the childlike disciples around Him. It is an exquisite joy to relieve the sufferings of the battlefield and hospital, or to carry a message of mercy to dying men; yet those circumstances are among the most painful that any person can know. Many are the burdens and sorrows that accompany a time of revival; yet who would forgo the holy joy of such a time?

Those who share the deep sorrows of Christ share all the joy of His work.

The inexpressible peace of God is ". . .shed abroad in our hearts" (Rom. 5:5), in a special manner when we grasp the privilege of suffering with our Lord. Anyone who attempts to endure suffering without God's peace will have a heavy burden to carry. Everyone who accepts Christ's unchanging soul Sabbath will indeed find that it brings many burdens, but the Lord himself becomes the burden-bearer. He sweetly carries us and our burdens too.

THE BAPTISM
OF THE SPIRIT

THE BAPTISM
OF THE SPIRIT

AVING always known that a Christian receives the Holy Spirit upon conversion, and that His guidance and power would be known in the believer's service and trials, I had not looked for any other special manifestation of His presence in my life. Yet I encountered many passages in the Bible that depicted conditions that were not fully met in my life, despite the fullness of my knowledge of pardon, adoption, and secure standing in Christ. My lack was still evident ten years after my conversion, when I received the wonderful inward cleansing by Christ's blood from all sin.

I had often read the Scripture promise, "Whosoever drinketh of the water that I shall give him shall never thirst; but the water that I shall give him shall be *in him* a well of water springing up into everlasting life" (John 4:14, italics added). This was not true in my experience, in the full meaning evidently intended by the words. There did not always flow freely and spontaneously from my heart "rivers of living water" (John 7:38). Too often the force-pump rather than the fountain would have represented my soul's condition. As I gazed into the mirror of God's Word, and as I meditated upon the glorious person of my Lord, I was often bowed in adoring love. But I had never come to "know" His Holy Spirit (John 14:17) in such fullness that I could realize His indwelling presence more genuinely than the visible person of Jesus.

I had read that as persons possessed by an evil spirit were led to do things far beyond their natural powers, so those filled with the Holy Spirit seemed to be enabled to serve God beyond their natural ability. I had read the charge that the Jews leveled against the apostles, saying that they were drunken because their behavior was so altered by the indwelling Holy Spirit (Acts 2:13); indeed, the apostle Paul said that the fullness of the Spirit resembled a drunkenness (Eph. 5:18). But as yet I had not been thus "filled with the Spirit," nor experienced what John the Baptist meant when he said that Christ "shall *baptize* you with the Holy Ghost and with fire" (Luke 3:16, italics added).

I was so ignorant, even in the matters of greatest importance to my spiritual welfare, that when I found inward cleansing and outward victory over sin—that faith which "overcometh the world" (1 John 5:4)—I did not understand that a far more glorious manifestation of God was yet to be given by His Holy Spirit. I scarcely noticed that *after* our Lord had breathed on His disciples and said, "Receive ye the Holy Ghost" (John 20:22), they had to wait many days in prayerful expectation for the full baptism of the Spirit. Indeed, I had advanced beyond the condition of those disciples who as yet had "not so much as heard whether there be any Holy Ghost" (Acts 19:2); but I had formed no conception of what the promised baptism with the Holy Spirit could be.

Deeply thankful for the privileges of sanctification through faith, realized a few months before, I one day met with a few Christians in a wooded area to wait for the baptism of the Holy Spirit. Except for a few hymns and brief prayers, the half-hour was spent in solemn silence. At length "there came a sound from heaven as of a rushing mighty wind" (Acts 2:2); no words of mine could better describe my impression of what was happening. Not a leaf or a blade of grass was stirred. All of nature was still. It was to our souls, rather than to our senses, that the Lord revealed himself by His Spirit. My whole being seemed unutterably full of the God in whom I had long believed. My senses could not bring such a consciousness as was now mine. I understood the supersensual visions of Isaiah, Ezekiel, and Paul, for no created thing was now so real to my soul as the Creator himself. It was an awful encounter, yet without terror. I lost no awareness of my senses, yet they were enwrapped in the sublime manifestation. A question that was put to me by another person in the group was answered as briefly as possible, so that I might lose no awareness of the heavenly presence of God, enwrapping and filling my being. I do not recall whether I then told anyone of what had happened. But, days afterward, when I rejoined my wife, she burst into tears as we met—before we had spoken a word—so marked was the change in my appearance.

I knew "songs in the night season" (Job 35:10, para.), and the living waters of Christ welling up within my heart upon the consciousness of waking each new day. An awe, sweet and not burdensome, shadowed my spirit. Every moment was filled with the presence of God. Nor did His presence leave me in the midst of the most engrossing occupations of each day. My whole life became a psalm of praise to Him.

This elevation of feeling naturally subsided after a season; but it left me with an inner consciousness of God that is well expressed by His words, "I will dwell in them, and walk in them" (2 Cor. 6:16). The scene of Christ dying upon the cross became more real to me than the senses could have made it. Without materializing before my physical sight, the holy countenance of Jesus—in His tender, suffering humanity lightened by the glory of His divinity—seems now to look down from the cross upon my audiences as I speak of His redemption for sinners.

It is painful to speak of these things. My poor words seem to cover them rather than reveal them. Would that the glorious reality could be conveyed to others!

After walking with little variation in this inward consciousness of the presence of God for about five years, I became aware of forms of selfishness, self-consciousness, self-dependence, and self-seeking that I had not before recognized. I felt like an Israelite in whose home were some defiling garments; by the grey morning light I had cleansed my dwelling and was without condemnation of conscience, but when the noontide sun poured in its rays, the evil things were discovered.

At once came the prayer of faith, "Cleanse me from this also, O my Savior!" And I had full confidence that it would be done.

Soon afterward, as I knelt in a large meeting of Christians waiting upon the Lord in silent prayer, I seemed to see Jesus sitting above me as a Refiner with fire. A flame seemed to pass through my soul, consuming the very evils about which I had been praying. I cannot find words more appropriate than those of Scripture to describe it:

> He shall sit as a refiner and purifier of silver: and he shall purify the sons of Levi, and purge them as gold and silver, that they may offer unto the LORD an offering in righteousness (Mal. 3:3).

To my surprise, I did not shrink from the fire, but gladly welcomed it as I seemed to look into the vividly revealed countenance of my tender Savior. I then understood in a far deeper sense then ever the words, "sanctify you wholly," for all of my sinful dross seemed to be burned up.

This occurred without much emotion, but it was wonderfully real to my soul. The event was followed by some of the most severe sorrows and temptations; but in them I was enabled to find deliverance by faith in Christ as my Refiner with fire.

About this time a few Christians from five denominations (among them six ministers) gathered for some evening meetings with the special object of finding out, through prayer, the full meaning of being "baptized with fire" and being "filled with the Spirit." They were walking in close communion with the Lord, in the paths of sanctification through faith, yet they knew they lacked a fullness of His blessing in the baptism of the Holy Spirit. Realizing that they were liable to interpret the Scriptures by their own educational predispositions, they resorted to continual prayer and waiting upon God, trusting that He himself would teach them the meaning of His Word.

The first evening, a well-known preacher of calm, intellectual habits who had been praying for the baptism for two months was so overwhelmed by the manifested presence of Jesus that he lay down with clasped hands and a look of heavenly joy for several hours. He later said, "I seemed mercifully shut out from intercourse with the world for a time, so that I might enjoy the presence of Jesus. After several hours I was able to whisper, 'The Lord whom you seek shall *suddenly* come to His temple; the rest I cannot tell." After a time, I whispered, 'It is the refiner's fire and the fuller's soap. I used to think it would be so dreadful, but it is so sweet." I remained thus till noon the next day, shut up alone with God, occasionally telling a little of the sweetness and the glory of the revelations of God's love, but so anxious not to miss a word of what He had to tell me that I did not speak much. I seemed to be ushered into the very presence of the Lord, as though I saw Him face to face and actually heard His voice. How I rejoiced to have that refining burn and burn, until it seemed to consume all the dross away. I could almost see the fan in His hand, thoroughly purging His threshing floor and separating the chaff from the wheat. "Oh, how I shall love to preach for Him now!"I exclaimed. "I always loved it, but now it will be so different and so sweet."I now loved everyone, even those whom it had seemed impossible to love. It was all love, love!

"It was hard to come back to the burden of common life again," he said, "but I knew that it was needful. I had to part with the vividness of these manifestations, as they would make the duties of ordinary life impossible."

The fact that all of this came to a person so

intellectual, so calm and reserved—and one whose life had manifested so much of the power of the Holy Spirit in God's service—seemed an unmistakable answer to our prayers, asking whether it is the privilege of every believer in the Lord Jesus to receive the *conscious, definite* baptism of the Holy Spirit similar to that on the Day of Pentecost. Now there rested upon each of us the responsibility to "tarry at Jerusalem" (Luke 24:49, para.), until we were baptized in a manner different from the *usual* degree of the Spirit's presence that most Christians realize. We were to receive His baptism to the thorough transformation, consciously and manifestly, of our entire beings.

An example of the results of this powerful baptism of the Spirit is found in the life story of a widely known physician. About twenty-four years ago, he assumed the medical care of a married woman in advanced consumption, who felt called of God to leave her home and go to his hospital. Her doctors expected her to die, as she had been bleeding in her lungs for twenty consecutive days. She could not speak above a whisper, and her death was expected momentarily. However, one day she spoke of having faith to be healed, and she asked her new physician to pray for her. Thinking her too weak to bear the emotional strain, he retired to his office and prayed that six more years of life should be given to her. She was almost instantly restored to her strength, so that in a few days she could travel by stagecoach in bitterly cold winter weather to her own home. She lived the six years that her doctor had claimed by faith—years of wonderful blessing in Christian work—and then died in triumph and hope.

During her illness, she described to the young physician how to obtain sanctification by faith. He heard her at first with intense prejudice, but was finally led to surrender his life to God. After four weeks of struggle and yielding to God, he surrendered to Christ the very last of all things that he was conscious of holding as his own. Then it seemed as though the heavens were opened; his soul intensely sensed the glory of God. But it soon seemed to vanish. "Why, Lord?" he cried.

"Because you are stubborn and willful," the answer came.

"Wherein, Lord?" he asked.

"You will not testify before others to the truth of sanctification by faith."

When he yielded at this point also, he was at once filled by a wonderful baptism of the Holy Spirit. He says that he has not had an unhappy day since, nor a day without the solemn consciousness of God. His life has been dedicated to the will of God. His heart and will have become a perpetual yes to every call of God. He always realizes that, even in the small details of life, God wills a certain course of action for him and shall communicate this to his waiting soul. When the many voices of self-will, prejudice, and enthusiasm are stilled, "a still small voice" (1 Kings 19:12), comes with satisfying certainty to his soul, saying, "This is the way; walk thou in it." The physician has found that inward peace and outward success are possible only by living in the perfect will of God.

Twenty-three years of close attention to this sacred teaching, with instantaneous obedience to the leadings of God, have made this man's spiritual senses to "grow by reason of use" (Heb. 5:14, para.). His walk with the Lord has imparted an indescribable gentleness and power to his very appearance and voice, joined to an irresistible authority. I have never seen the character of the head of a family so clearly impressed upon the activities of a household as with this man's. I have never seen an unkind expression or heard a harsh word in his house. The very atmosphere of the place is filled with the pervading presence of the love of God. There are simplicity, restfulness, and hidden power in the religious activities of the household which have brought a spirit of continuous revival to those who visit it. Probably thousands of people have been converted or lifted to a higher experience of the love of God over the past twenty-three years in this holy, beautiful home. Weary souls find its soothing influences so sweet that, like the Lotus-eaters, they can barely force themselves away. Travelers who stop by chance for a night of rest will seek the first opportunity to return. (The casual reader may think these statements exaggerated; but those who have shared the privileges of this household know it is as I have described.) For this physician, the baptism of the Holy Spirit has not been a transient joy but an abiding grace for nearly a quarter of a century, bearing fruit to God such as few of God's children have been able to know.

It is not unusual for this wonderful baptism of the Holy Spirit to come when the believer first begins walking in the light; but in most cases that I have observed, believers have pursued a life of perfect trust for some time before they have received the transforming baptism of the Spirit. Hundreds of Christians have told me of the suddenness of the baptism, and of its lasting results in their character and labors. They also testify of their certainty of receiving the baptism.

If a man had been born blind and grew up without ever seeing the light, and was suddenly cured, he might ask upon seeing a candle, "Is this it?" Or again, when he saw the moon, "Is this it?" But if such a man was to see the sun for the first time, he would ask no questions, but exclaim, "*This is it!*" Thus, I can imagine that those who have not received the baptism of the Spirit may wonder whether they have received it. But those who have once experienced the Holy Spirit in His fullness will say, "*This is it!*"

Pray for this. Trust God's promises for this. Wait in holy expectation for this—if need be, as long as Jesus' first disciples waited. And when you have received the Spirit's baptism, ask that it be renewed on every occasion of need. Have faith to be always filled with the Spirit, whether in His mighty, rushing power or in His gentle, dewlike quietness, to possess and mold your heart for Christ.